A Unique Approach to
Family Counseling

Other books by Elisabeth Lukas:

Meaning and Suffering

The Therapist and the Soul

In the series
Viktor Frankl's Living Logotherapy:

Understanding *Man's Search for Meaning*:
Reflections on Viktor Frankl's Logotherapy

A Unique Approach to Family Counseling:
Logotherapy, Crisis, and Youth

Stillness and Concentration:
Logotherapy Applied to Tinnitus and Chronic Illness

Meaningful Living:
Introduction to Logotherapy Theory and Practice

A Unique Approach to Family Counseling:

Logotherapy, Crisis, and Youth

Elisabeth Lukas

Translated by
Joseph Fabry, Bianca Hirsch, Howard Smith, & James O'Meara

Edited by Charles McLafferty, Jr.

Book 2: *Viktor Frankl's Living Logotherapy* series

Purpose
Research
Charlottesville, Virginia

Published by Purpose Research, Box 5032, Charlottesville, Virginia 22905 USA
http://PurposeResearch.com   charles@purposeresearch.com
Back cover photograph © 2014 Charles McLafferty, Jr.
Cover design, layout, and typesetting by Purpose Research

The following were originally translated by Joseph Fabry and published in *The international forum for logotherapy* (Fabry, J. and/or Hutzell, R., eds.): Chapter 1, "The message of logotherapy to parents and teachers"; Chapter 2, "Meaningful education"; Chapter 3, "The meaning of children's play"; Chapter 6, "Love and work in Frankl's view of human nature"; Chapter 8, "Meaning-centered family counseling"; Chapter 9, "Logotherapeutic crisis intervention: A case history"; and Chapter 10, "Self-help and crisis intervention."

The following keynote addresses were translated by Joseph Fabry, Howard Smith, and James O'Meara and published privately by Elisabeth Lukas in *Psychotherapy with dignity* (1992): Chapter 4, "Youth: A continuous search for meaning" (1986); Chapter 5, "'Family first': The meaning of love and family" (1988); Chapter 7, "From a wrong idea to the Desert Storm: The logotherapeutic approach to conflict resolution" (1991); and Chapter 11, "Personal attitudes and the preservation of life" (1987). Chapter 6, "Love and work" has also been published by the author in *Psychological Ministry* (1995) as well as Lukas, E. (2015). *The doctor and the soul*. Charlottesville: Purpose Research (reprinted with permission). Poems after each chapter are from Lukas, E. (1992). *Meaningful lines: Logophilosophical wisdom* (Hirsch, B. & Fabry, J., trans.). Berkeley: Institute of Logotherapy Press.

All quotes and excerpts are believed to be fair use.

For more information about the work of Elisabeth Lukas around the world, please visit the Lukas Archives: http://elisabeth-lukas-archiv.de
For more information about training in logotherapy and existential analysis search for "Viktor Frankl Institute" and "Elisabeth Lukas Archive" on the web.

ISBN: 978-1-948523-21-9 (Hardcover)
978-1-948523-01-1 (Paperback)

Library of Congress Control Number: 2019951513

9 8 7 6 5 4 3 2 1

Contents

Foreword vii

1. The Message of Logotherapy to Parents and Teachers 1

2. Meaningful Education 9

3. The Meaning of Children's Play 19

4. Youth: A Continuous Search for Meaning. 23

5. "Family First": The Meaning of Love and Family 37

6. Love and Work in Frankl's View of Human Nature. 51

7. From a Wrong Idea to the Desert Storm:
    The Logotherapeutic Approach to Conflict Resolution 65

8. Meaning-Centered Family Counseling 87

9. Logotherapeutic Crisis Intervention: A Case History 101

10. Self-Help and Crisis Intervention 107

11. Personal Attitudes and the Preservation of Life 119

Foreword

Viktor Frankl (1905–1997) lived a remarkable life. Even as a teenager, he was a deep thinker, embracing the philosophy of existentialism in his thinking; the nihilistic trend of the time was a deep weight on a 16-year-old struggling with the meaning of life. It was at the end of this period that he developed his well-known definition of "God," that even his atheist patients could accept: "God is the partner of our most intimate soliloquies."

It is hard to pin down exactly what traits made his life so remarkable, though some part must be attributed to his innate curiosity. In his "first life" (as he called it) he was a member of Sigmund Freud's circle and published an article in Freud's journal. But the two had a falling out, and Frankl found his way into Adler's group of thinkers. After being expelled from Adler's group for expressing his ideas, Frankl continued to explore what made the individual unique—what was it that was missing in the current thinking?

After earning his medical degree, Viktor Frankl served as a psychiatrist on a mental ward, honing his theory and his practice. He gave hope to unemployed individuals during the Great Depression and helped students approaching graduation from gymnasium (high school) to face a dreaded exit exam rather than commit suicide.

His "first life" ended when he entered the concentration camps with a manuscript sewn into his jacket, a completed book that outlined in detail his well-developed theory, which he called *logotherapy*. Even that manuscript was lost, but Frankl never lost hope; if not for himself, then for the sake of the other prisoners who were also struggling. In his darkest moments, he reported occasional visions that sustained him—of his wife and family members, or of the work that lay ahead of him, a unique task that only he could fulfill. He visualized himself standing in the Medical School of Vienna auditorium, giving lectures about logotherapy. He survived typhus by trying to recreate the ideas from his lost book on scraps of paper while everyone else was asleep.

Thankfully, Frankl survived the horrors of the Holocaust and entered his "second life." He had lost everything—his wife, his family, his work—and at one point considered suicide. But there was work to be done, meaning to be fulfilled, and, as he reported, he gradually regained his humanity. Our world continues to be enriched by the second life of Viktor Frankl.

What remains is the question that Frankl adddressed: What is it that makes each person unique? His response established a foundation based on a dimensional viewpoint of the person. Our traditional theories, he said, do a very good job of conveying an understanding of the physical and emotional/intellectual aspects of the person, which he termed the dimensions of soma and psyche, respectively. Frankl did not eschew the theories that incorporated these dimensions; he honored and respected them. But, he pointed out, soma and psyche are what the human being shares with animals. The human being has another aspect, which had been largely ignored by previous theorists. In English, Frankl called this "the noëtic dimension," the human spirit. He defined it as "that which separates us from animals" and pointed out that it is in this dimension that the human being has conscience, responsibility, choice, free will, the defiant power of the human spirit, and self-transcendence. It is precisely in the noëtic dimension that the human being comes to know him- or herself as a unique person, one that has no replacement, and to whom Life calls with a unique task that no one else can fulfill.

About Elisabeth Lukas

Elisabeth Lukas is arguably a pre-eminent student of Viktor Frankl. In college, Lukas attended a lecture by Frankl that transformed her life. She became a clinical psychologist while empirically validating Frankl's theory with her Logotest. Lukas has tirelessly helped and uplifted clients of all social classes, incomes, levels of illness, and types of disability. She has advocated for meaning possibilites of aging adults at the last stages of life as well as the very youngest at the beginning of life. She has trained thousands of logotherapists at the South German Institute for Logotherapy and Existential Analysis and, later, the Training Institute for Logotherapy (ABILE) as well as through workshops and courses at universities and conferences around the world.

Lukas has a unique imprimatur that is relevant when reading this book. After training a group of logotherapists, she charges them with the need to *live logotherapy*. It is not enough to learn about the theory, it must be lived uniquely. Each person is unique; each of us must find our own way to harvest the meaning potentials available in each moment ("the meaning of the moment") and to orient to the magnetic pull of what Frankl called "Ultimate Meaning." In the same manner, these books are not "absolute truth" or "the gospel" of logotherapy—Frankl, in fact, was deeply concerned about those who parrotted his every word. Rather, the inisights of Lukas (and Frankl) serve as guideposts to each of us to consider as we find our own unique path of meaning.

About this series

Over the years, Lukas has written more than 50 books, which have been translated into 19 languages. She has given keynote addresses and lectures at numerous universities and conferences, including many of the World Congresses of Logotherapy. Her writings have been translated into English for print in books and journals, particularly *The international forum for logotherapy: Journal of search for meaning*. For years, I have wanted to collect these writings in a book form. I am grateful for the support of Elisabeth Lukas and the Elisabeth Lukas Archive, as well as others who have given so unselflishly of their time and energy to help move this project forward.

The first book, *Understanding Man's Search for Meaning: Reflections on Viktor Frankl's logotherapy*, contains some of the most insightful and profound expansions of logotherapy into the problems of our time. Many of these chapters are drawn from keynote addresses to World Congresses of

Logotherapy. Until now, most of the English versions have been privately published, though some have appeared in the *International forum for logotherapy*.

This volume, *A unique approach to family counseling: Logotherapy, crisis, and youth* focuses on the application of logotherapy in families and relationships. It includes articles from the *International forum*, book chapters, and keynote speeches.

The third volume has two parts: The first part of this book is a translation of *Stillness and concentration: Logotherapy for tinnitus and chronic diseases*. The rest of the book contains articles and presentations that fall broadly under the topic of "psychotherapy with dignity."

A new edition of *Meaningful living: Introduction to logotherapy theory and practice* is the fourth book in the series. The first part is a revision of the 1984 classic, *Meaningful living: Logotherapeutic guide to health*. The second part adds an article by Elisabeth Lukas and Bianca Hirsch that was originally published in the *Comprehensive handbook of psychotherapy, vol. 3*. Many of the cases summarized in the article can be found in more detail in the original text of *Meaningful living*, and are cross-referenced throughout. This archival article also documents the history of logotherapy as of 2002.

To the extent possible, these books have been edited for a new generation of logotherapists. Sentences have been restructured whenever possible to use inclusive language (including sex, race, culture, and gender identity) and to minimize labeling (e.g., "person with an addiction disorder" instead of "addict") in accordance with the *Publication Manual of the American Psychological Association* (6th ed). Further, the translation of these concepts from German into English occasionally resulted in difficult-to-understand passages, and these have been revised and even rewritten. If, as a result of this work, meaning has been lost or changed, that is solely my fault, and for that I take full responsibility. Hopefully, the inherent meaning will shine through when English words are inadequate to express it.

It is hoped that these books will serve to kindle interest in the meaning possibilities available to all of us, and in so doing ignite the flames of meaning among those who sense there is something more to life than having possessions, money, a beautiful home, a prestigious position, and a multitude of friends. To those enduring long periods of unemployment during the Great Depression nearly a century ago, Frankl noted that the problem wasn't a lack of money, but a lack of meaning.

To each reader, no matter at what stage in life, regardless of your setbacks, failures, and fate, there awaits a purpose that only you can fulfill, one for which you were created. It is the discovery of, orientation to, and *action on* this possibility that brings meaning. Even a few minutes a day pursuing this unique life mission will result in a harvest of positive fruits and help you to build a monument of meaning that can never be taken away… in time or in eternity.

Charles McLafferty, Jr.
University of Virginia
June, 2019

CHAPTER 1

The Message of Logotherapy
to Parents and Teachers

Parents, educators, physicians, therapists, and politicians worry about the development of the next generation. They cannot take quite seriously those child-adult scatterbrains, yet they must do just that. They wonder what is wrong with them, who have discredited Freud and Adler by appropriating to themselves all the privileges of sexuality and power without ever becoming happy. Gone are the suppressed, subdued, shy youngsters with their inferiority complexes as described (and psychologically interpreted) before the two World Wars. The new generations are largely self-confident, unrestrained, reckless, brutal, and vulnerable to suicide and drug addiction. At least, this is the way today's young people are tagged; their symptoms are characterized as those of a decaying society. The conflicts between the generations are growing, their world views are clashing, and mutual criticism manifests itself in discord and violence. All this has been sufficiently described—the anarchism, the juvenile delinquency, the alternative lifestyles, and the furious threats by frustrated parents along with the helpless shoulder shrugging of confused significant others.

Young people running wild, dissatisfied with the world and themselves, set on changing the world, yet unable to change even themselves—how did it come about? As psychologists, we traditionally place responsibility on external circumstances, the loss of natural instincts, the breakdown of traditions; however, few of us acknowledge that we have significantly contributed to the situation.

For many decades, we have undermined the basis of educational practice. Every few years, we have instructed and confused parents and teachers by proclaiming a new educational style without knowing how these experiments would work out. We have designed a crazy human image, the model of a monster either pushed blindly by its drives or a person hopelessly suppressed by society—in either case, a creature unable to take care of itself and in need of protection.

In addition, we have psychologically supported the emancipation of mothers and helped millions of children to achieve a high standard of living while feeling lonesome and neglected. We have coddled this growing army of small psychopaths by a special kind of education-via-the-media—by exposing them to models of brutality on television and through video games until they muddle up the normal and abnormal, the valuable and worthless, because their sense of values is fundamentally disturbed. As psychologists, we have confounded liberty and antiauthoritarianism, blurred the difference between children's laziness and resistance to excessive demands, and found classic excuses for any sort of aberration. (The traumas of childhood justify such behavior; the parents are the scapegoats.) The most fashionable scapegoat, however, is society itself, whose structure (whatever this is supposed to mean) is made responsible for all mental ills of our day. The only group whose responsibility is not discussed is that of the people involved.

EDUCATION FOR RESPONSIBILITY

As a professional psychologist I can afford to make this criticism. And I can also address myself to those parents who suffer just as much as their children but bear the brunt of the insecurity which we, the "experts," have created. In my practice, I have talked with hundreds of desperate parents and learned that everybody they asked for counsel had different advice.

The concepts on which such counsel is based differ even among the counseling services. Institutions with psychoanalytic orientations are at odds with those devoted to behaviorism, school officials differ with educational counselors, physicians have other ideas than therapists, and customs taught in the homes of our children clash with academic theory. In the middle are the parents, caught in the cross fire of the pontifications of the various experts, abandoned in their frustration of not knowing how to handle the children who get out of hand and laugh at all those abortive educational efforts. Young adults tell the counselor that their parents "are *so old*"; and counselors nod weightily in agreement, fearful lest they lose the confidence of their clients, not wanting want them to put the counselor in the same boat as their parents.

We do not need theories of dysfunctions caused by unconscious traumas, repressed sex symbols, and inferiority complexes; we need *education for responsibility*. We need an education that directs the younger generation toward meaning and values; just as importantly, we need an education that directs parents toward teaching and living meaning and values. The crisis of our time can be seen as primarily educational, a failure to educate people so they see themselves as full human beings.

The last generations in Germany can look back on extraordinary accomplishments: They have rebuilt a war-devastated land into a flowering economic paradise. Even threats of inflation and unemployment have been unable to shatter the total economic edifice. But building up provides more meaning than inheriting its results, because building up is goal-directed and endows the effort with meaning, whereas inheriting provides neither goal nor meaning. On the contrary; fortunes that fall in our laps are valued little. The young cannot accept as meaningful goals homes that are already built and paid for or large cars standing in their parents' garage; they cannot derive their youthful ideas from the strength of the Euro. To repeat, I am not going to point an accusing finger at parents—they are not supermen and superwomen and, for the most part, they do what they can for their children.

If accusations must be made at all, they must be directed against my colleagues. Why, in all those decades, did they not tell parents to give their children a value orientation? All problems of toddlers and all crises of puberty have been talked to death in popular discussions. But parents have not been prepared for the most important step in their children's lives when the young must prepare themselves to find their own tasks and challenges—for this pivotal moment of searching for meaning in the maturing process!

AREAS OF BLOCKED MEANINGS

In fact, the opposite is true. In three areas of education the views of the contemporary experts have actually stifled the orientation toward meaning and values. Let me briefly discuss the three areas:

The first is *accomplishment*. It is risky today for a psychologist to use this word at all, because of all the negative connotations heaped on it by experts. Slogans such as "achievement pressure" and "excessive demands" on the "overworked" child have made such inroads that teachers are scared of students and parents are scared of their children. "Don't ask for achieve-ment" was drummed into teachers, and "don't accomplish" into students. Those who study are ridiculed for their ambition, those who work are seen as selling out to "the Establishment," and those who save money are pitied as bourgeois. How can a generation with such a philosophy of life under-stand the constructive work of their parents? How can young individuals feel satisfaction and pride in workmanship in their own work; indeed, how can they begin to be motivated to seek fulfillment in work—even in hobbies—if everything that results in human accomplishment has been devalued and derided?

The second area for which experts have to accept responsibility is the *concept of the group*. For a time, only sociological groups seemed to exist, the individual did not count. The group dictates to its members; it pressures and absorbs them. Woe to those who try to break out, woe to those who don't cultivate an unkempt look! They are not "in." Smoking, alcohol, are drugs are part of the group identity. If you are not good in bed you lose the approval of the group. If you don't join in ridiculing authorities the group laughs at you. I have seen parents asking the counselor for advice because their "abnormal" child loves classical music, causing trouble with their peers. A young person who is not familiar with the latest bands and music trends does not "fit." What madness to subordinate all individuality and interests, talents, views, and meaningful satisfactions to an imaginary group that consists of conformists. How ardently have the psychologists and educators drilled into parents that they should buckle in uncritically to The Group: If all children read comic books, the parents must not withhold such literature from *their* children; if all classmates read detective stories until midnight, so must their child. How are these young people in later life to find their own personal style, their own tasks, the much-vaunted self-actualization? How can they mature into that unique and unexchangeable identity that every person should and must attain, if they have nobody and nothing to orient to but "the group"?

The third area in which our experts have sowed dangerous misconceptions concerns *freedom*.

The shout for freedom among the young is as loud as their concept of freedom is false. True freedom demands the highest measure of responsibility. It does not allow the chaos of reckless acts, regardless of consequences. Freedom does not mean *to do what you want* but *to want what is called for*. I do not mean a want dictated by outer authority but one called for by the inner authority of the conscience, which is responsive to what in logotherapy is called *the meaning of the moment*. Free are those who include themselves in a structure they recognize; unfree are those who reject any kind of structure.

In the mistaken belief that they can win freedom by throwing out rules, disregarding laws, and overstepping limitations, young people frequently succumb to dependencies they don't even recognize. The conking out of a smartphone or laptop can be a catastrophe for a weekend because they have become so dependent on it that they don't know what to do with their free time. They only know what *not* to do with it, they know their freedom *from*, namely from work, tasks, responsibleness.

True freedom means a freedom *to*—productive creation, affirmation of somebody or something, completion of a self-chosen task. Many of the young are far removed from such a concept, accepting dependencies on the most ludicrous fashion fads and demonstrating their desire for freedom by revolt and violence. Here, too, educational help should be available for even the very young so that the ability for free and goal-directed decisions is combined with an awareness of responsibleness.

PREVENTIVE EDUCATION

These comments are intended to outline the central concerns of modern counseling. Frankl's logotherapy is psychotherapy, philosophy, and anthropology combined, but it also includes valuable educational aspects. To reveal the meaning crisis of our younger generations in all its aspects is not enough. What is needed is to offer parents and children genuine help and thereby reduce—if not prevent—the worldwide spread of the existential vacuum.

As psychotherapists, we are easy victims of the illusion that we can heal all ills. True healing would mean that no one needs us. We like to fight fire instead of fighting arson. We play doctor for sick minds without being able to protect the healthy ones. We do not acknowledge the proverbial wisdom that an ounce of prevention is better than a pound of cure; if we did, we would give pedagogy, rather than pathology, our priority.

A mutual relationship exists between education and mental health. Educational counseling institutions have long discovered that, to be successful, parents need to be aware of the therapeutic resources of the human spirit. It is time for psychotherapeutic institutions to recognize that preventive education for our children and young adults is mandatory. While the psychotherapist tries to renormalize one human being, two others lose their grip on life because their education (in the widest sense of the word) is insufficient. Most psychotherapies, starting from the sick and abnormal, present a reductionistic caricature of the healthy human being. Psychotherapists will have to learn to concern themselves with healthy persons.

There is only one contemporary psychotherapeutic theory that provides the necessary spiritual underpinnings—a view of humankind that starts from the multidimensionality of the healthy person and deducts from it what the sick person needs. This theory does not deduce from the clinical history of compulsive sexual neurotics an all-dominating instinctive drive in the healthy person; nor does it conclude from conditioned abnormal reactions of patients that the normal individual is a learning machine without a will. Viktor Frankl's logotherapy finally puts an end to psychological and sociological determinism that forever chains human beings to their childhood experiences and sociological environments.

It took psychotherapy half a century to restore to human beings what they always knew in their unconscious: that they have freedom of choice, responsibleness, and a will to meaning. This is the direction in which we must counsel parents today, for the sake of their children's future. This is the direction in which we must guide the young if we want to lighten their burden. Let us never forget: Our investments in an education toward developing a full human being are the premiums for the only existing life insurance for a meaningful life.

Father and mother
create a child.

But in reality
they are not
creators of a new human being
but a testimony
of a new miracle
of becoming human.

Because father and mother
pass on their physical–
psychic heritage
—not their spirit!

Elisabeth Lukas

CHAPTER 2

Meaningful Education

What is the significance of education? Is education responsible if we fail or are successful in our development? Some psychologists assert this as an oversimplification. But education can be assigned only one-third of the success or failure. The other two-thirds come from our genetic make-up and our own contribution—how we manage what we have received through genes and education.

Although education accounts for only part of our development, the importance of a meaningful education cannot be denied. First, the influence of that one-third is important and, secondly, we live in a time when educators feel tremendously insecure. My suggestions here are to encourage educators to support well-developed young people in the development they have achieved and to enable troubled young people to reach their full potential.

Educational texts tell us that children need love; thus, that parents need to bring up their children with love. True enough, but children also need the capacity *to be* loved. Hence, parents should educate their children not only *with* love but *for* love. Here we proceed from the level of advising parents and teachers to help children and students to meet their needs, to the next-higher level in which youngsters are equipped with qualities that will help them in situations in which they are needed.

An example will illustrate the difference between the two levels. How, for instance, can brutality and excesses in football and other sports be prevented? How can spectators be protected from dangerous aggressive acts by fanatics? Many politicians and educators offer unruly children alternatives to gratify their needs—fan clubs, youth rallies, workshops... even their own small sports arenas in which they can abreact their excess energies in a supposedly "meaningful" manner.

What is overlooked is that meaningful abreacting is not possible. All abreacting is a discharge into "anywhere." But "anywhere" is not a meaningful goal even if its target is a harmless surrogate. For example, if people quarrel with a friend, and then hurry home and slam the door rather than kick a dog, they have chosen a harmless target because the door does not feel the pain the dog would feel. But slamming doors is not a meaningful goal.

The model project has another flaw: Its only concern is gratifying an urge. Whatever our children and young adults need, the educators say, let them have it. And if they still don't develop normally and need something else—let them have that, too. By this method we never get beyond supplying their wants and needs; however, we don't educate them toward *being needed*. This, however, would meet their most profound need—the wish to be useful to others and the world.

Educator Eduard Spanger once said that the most fundamental difference in our world views is between drifting and feeling responsible. What he meant, no doubt, was that it is not enough to show young people in which direction they might drift without doing harm; they have to accept responsibility and learn to pick up the reins themselves—even against the pressures of drives and needs.

Responsibility means, for instance, after a quarrel with a friend to neither smash the door nor kick the dog (both of which have nothing to do with the quarrel) but to search for compromise and reconciliation.

Therefore, meaningful education will teach children two central guidelines: (a) aggressive urges must not be directed against others, least of all against the innocent and (b) not everything that's easy is permitted.

I start with these guidelines because there are two psychological views that have confused some educators.

REPRESSION THEORY

The first view is *repression theory* (advanced by the followers of depth psychology), which states that all repressed aggression and frustration surface as neuroses or psychosomatic illnesses. This view leads to the conclusion that it is preferable to fight, curse, shout, and kick (regardless of the target), than to swallow anger, because "stuffing" anger will have pathologic consequences. Hence unruly soccer fans, who beat up people in the street if the "wrong" club has won, act "correctly" in this model of psychohygiene: They don't swallow their anger.

Here is a case history of a patient that illustrates repression theory:

One of my patients had been plagued by diarrhea. Her physician first sent her to a psychotherapist, who explored her childhood to find the trauma that would explain everything. Indeed, he discovered that she, as a 6-year-old, had lost her beloved father. She said she was so close to her father that at the moment of his death in the hospital she, at home, sensed the crisis and broke out in tears. The therapist thereupon revealed to her that she must have felt massive anger against her father because he had deserted her. The repressed anger had caused her illness. He prescribed scream therapy: She should put herself back into her childhood and express her anger in screaming, thus "dissolving" the trauma. Six months of screaming did not help, and she sought my advice.

My first aim was to prevent a new trauma, this time in the dimension of the spirit, and not in the psyche—a misinterpretation of humanness. True humanness self-transcends and is not satisfied with self-actualization (with or without screaming). It searches for self-transcending values it wishes to serve, not merely for egocentric wishes on whose fulfillment it wants to *be* served.

I told the woman: "If as a child you really had such affection for your father, you felt at the moment of his death not that he *wanted* to desert you, but that fate tore him from you; that he *could not* be with you any longer; therefore there was no reason to be angry at him. If there was truly love between you and him, then you sensed that this love did not end with death—sensed this in the same way you sensed his death. Indeed this love lives on to this day. There is no reason to assume that your illness is caused by repressed anger."

She wiped off her tears and, relieved, confessed that all along she had felt the scream therapy was unjustified because, as I suspected, she still had loving memories of her father.

As for her intestinal troubles, it turned out that they were inherited; as far back as her great-grandmother, family members had suffered from it. Her father's grandmother had suffered from acute cramps during her wedding, and was more absent than present, according to chuckling family lore.

This example reflects a widespread antieducational attitude. If something isn't right with children, parents did something wrong, such as daring to die at the wrong time. We fail to see that parents are not responsible for everything—our children are exposed to many influences. We cannot "shape" our children; they shape themselves. Parents and teachers only provide the tools for them to use their inner resources.

Hence talk about "accepting yourself as you are" is the same nonsense as the talk about "saying everything openly." None of us IS a certain way, we all live in the tension between the *be* and the *ought*, as Frankl expressed it. All of us can act differently at any time, we can become a bit more perfect if we want to, instead of *being as we are*. We cannot simply spill out anything that passes in our mind, or do anything without considering the effect on others, or else we could condone any emotion-loaded knife battle; and words, too, can cut like knives.

So educators must not get misled by the specter of the repression theory—not every instance of self-control is repression. Only animals lack self-control and responsibility. Children are not animals; they have a conscience and thus can veto any unleashing of emotions and aggressions that follow the idea that "Never mind the others, what counts is that I got rid of what bothered me." We can't get rid of the voice of conscience no matter how much anger we have screamed out of our system. A psychotherapy that creates a conflict with one's conscience is only a prescription for an existential crisis.

THE "EASY WAY"

The second important guideline for educators reminds us that not everything that is easy is permissible. This guideline is denied not by the repression theory of depth psychology but by current family therapy. According to it, the victim is as guilty as the wrongdoer—indeed, there are no victims, only carriers of symptoms. If a boy in school does not defend himself, it's his own fault when children attack him. If he grimaces in anguish, which makes the other children laugh, he actually has provoked his own torture. It's that simple. The whole class is summarily tagged as being dysfunctional, and the helpless boy who does not know how to defend himself is considered the carrier of the dysfunction in that class.

Here again, we see an oversimplified portrait of the human being: Those who are angry will hit or scream to get rid of the anger, and those who have an opportunity will attack because it's easy. The woman who walks by herself at night in the park should not be surprised to get raped. And parents who meet their children's every wish should not be surprised if the children exploit them.

Is this point of view morally defensible? Or is it not true that in every situation we are responsible for our actions—attacks, rapes, exploitations—whether these are made easy or not? What is easy to do is not necessarily permissible, else one could strangle every baby in its crib... because it's easy.

Here is an example from my practice. A wife who habitually humiliated her husband explained: "He accepts everything. If he would threaten to leave me I would respect him more, but I can do what I please with him and he will always be agreeable."

I answered: "If he is always agreeable, then it's *you* who has to change. If you can do with him as you please, shouldn't you do what you *ought* to do? And the same goes for your relationship with all the people you meet.

Shouldn't you demand of yourself the best possible conduct in your marriage rather than request from your husband a worse conduct, namely that he threaten you in return? True, another husband may well have left you, but the fact that yours didn't may not be a sign of weakness but of love. Your conduct, however, doesn't show strength but lack of love."

"He should restrain me," she called out.

"No," I replied, "the burden of restraint rests with you. If you work on yourself, you can grow into a loving woman, worthy of her man who, despite your provocations, remains kind to you." My words resonated with her because in her heart she knew full well that the abuse of her husband could not be shoved aside by saying "It's his fault."

Children, too, test their limits; they often know exactly what they can get away with when they visit Grandma but not when with parents or teachers. They should not get stuck in this infantile state, which even a trained dog can attain. They should gradually reach a state in which they no longer ask what the rewards or punishments are, but what is right or wrong—a state in which the reaction of others does not decide their actions but rather their own conscience.

Another example from my practice: I asked a couple of quarrelsome siblings to tell me two things they did not like to do. They said "doing homework" and "washing dishes." I asked them which they would choose if I requested them to do one of the two.

"That's mean," they replied.

"You see," I said, "if you make people choose between two negative alternatives, they are forced to do something they don't want, whichever way they choose. If you attack others, they have to choose between two negative alternatives: fight back though they don't really want to, or run away. They are either angry enough to respond to your aggression with aggressiveness or "stupid" enough to capitulate. They want to be neither aggressive nor stupid but you allowed no third alternative." We discussed this awhile and they saw the possibility in future disagreements to give their friends "better alternatives."

Our education has to show that the guilty party is the aggressor or blackmailer, regardless of how the victim reacts; just because the victim makes it easy for the wrongdoer does not justify the aggressive behavior.

DENIAL OF LIFE

In this discussion of meaningful education I have stressed a strengthening of the capacity to love and to overcome aggressive potential and self-centered tendencies. We don't know what crises our children will face, but we know they will face them. Humankind now faces great dangers. Unconcern, narcissistic self-interest, and indifference toward nature have produced massive pollution of the environment. AIDS can spread only because of *lack* of love—although tied to the act of love—because those who love their partners will not expose them to a deadly infection merely for the sake of a few moments of lust. Here we are at a crossroads.

Love—does it mean to love me or others? Being human—does it mean satisfying my own wishes all the way to self-actualization or does it mean orientation toward meaning and values all the way to self-transcendence? "Desirable self-image" is more than identity. True, identity describes more than our unique qualities; it also includes our attitudes toward them. But our desirable self-image goes beyond that. It includes awareness of our humanness: whether we are driven or responsible, make demands or fulfill tasks, seek pleasure or pursue meaning, see ourselves as victims of chance or as cocreators of an unfathomable but divine plan.

There is today a disease more infectious and deadly than AIDS: the disease of denial of life. It is characterized by a flight into the world of simulation. Denial of life seduces a person to drop into an unreal, dreamy, stupefied world which does not require problem-solving because problems are either not noted or seem to solve themselves. In the TV and video world one watches passively—slips into a dreamland, into the shoes of the hero who vanquishes every foe, into the bedrooms of attractive and willing sexual partners; enjoys the stories of fictitious creatures; faces life and death situations far removed from our own. In the world of computer gaming, one chases nonexistent foes, sinks ships of phantom enemies, plays tennis without rackets. In the world of rock music, one is submerged in deafening noise drowning out the real questions of life. Dancing to this music is no longer creative but an opportunity to not-think, to not-respond, to be submersed in a din of nothingness. Stronger still is denial of life in the world of drugs: A snort, an injection, a toke, a pill leads to immersion into a fantasy world which mimics the real.

In this kind of contentment—or, rather, this being content with simulation and nonreality—the self is only watching and passively experiencing, not acting and functioning. And when it comes to a confrontation with reality, requiring decision and acting, the emptiness of a meaningless existence is revealed. The unlived life exacts its tribute, often in the form of despair and suicide.

If we wish to protect our young, our education will aim at strengthening the capacity to love, as well as the capacity to suffer. Persons able to suffer do not escape into a pain-free world of simulation when facing suffering; they confront it and possibly help ban it from the world, the real world. If confrontation and elimination is not possible, they accept it and courageously integrate it into their lives, the *real* world. They do not need to deny life with its unavoidable suffering, if they are able to accept it. The capacity to tolerate suffering makes them unassailable and, at the same time, willing to act when necessary.

An educator will not purposely create suffering, of course, to strengthen the students' capacity to suffer. Neither true love nor fateful suffering can be artificially produced; they come as experience, and our task is to *respond* to love and to accept unavoidable suffering. We are given many chances to learn that there are different ways to respond to "fate." If a child loses a ball, we do not need to promise a bigger and more beautiful ball to pacify the crying child, to save the child from "trauma." We can instead search with the child for new attitudes toward the loss of a ball—a lesson that may well be a model for more serious deprivations. Such attitudes may take the form of "perhaps another child will find the ball and enjoy the find." Or, "Now I know what to buy for your birthday and you can help me pick out a new ball."

These minor educational opportunities also offer the chance to strengthen the ability to suffer if, for example, a family member suffers a serious misfortune. It might be a misfortune that can be overcome only by a joint effort requiring the rallying of all forces—uniting what was separated, comforting what was painful.

Education to a meaningful life requires education to courage and love. Only *with* courage can we educate children *to* courage—including the courage to bear unavoidable blows of fate—and only *with* love can we educate *to* love—including love for life.

Faith
is more than
"building illusions,"
more than
"blind faith in God,"
more than
simply "not knowing."

All this is not enough.

Faith,
that means
"understanding yourself,"
often means
"uniting body and spirit,"
simply means
to know:
Everything has its meaning.

Elisabeth Lukas

CHAPTER 3

The Meaning of Children's Play

The meaning of children's play may found in an activity that allows them to be creative or skillful, or in an experience they can share with others or in some way relate to their lives.

Toy manufacturers tend to produce games that provide little opportunity for children to find meaning: dogs that bark at the push of a button, battleships that sink an enemy, race tracks for fancy toy cars that chase each other in circles, space creatures that can be taken apart and put together again. These toys provide fun but are soon forgotten. How much more lasting is the interest of a child in a simple boat carved from a piece of wood and floated in a pond. The child knew what the carving was for, it had a goal in view, and found satisfaction in having accomplished a self-chosen task.

Children are often as alienated from meaning in play as their parents are alienated from meaning in work. Such children feel bored; they rebel and become destructive—on their belongings at home, at school, in the neighborhood, and on other people. A German magazine featured an article, "What to do when children hit parents." A professor of psychology advised the threatened parent: "Quickly hand the child a vase and let him smash it against the wall. That will abreact his aggression."

Such advice is based on the concept of the human being as a reservoir of pent-up emotions which must be released at any price when the dam is threatening to burst. This concept of the human being completely disregards the dimension of the spirit and thus reduces the individual to a helpless bundle of repressed drives.

In our counseling center, we tried an experiment with six extremely aggressive children who caused their parents great worries. These children slit open the belly of a new teddy bear, tore the leg off of a doll, scribbled and crumpled up the pages of an illustrated book, let air out of balls, smashed toy cars—children who simply did not know how to play but only how to destroy and to throw away the ruined toy.

We asked the parents to collect the pieces of the broken toys and bring them along to the first session. To the children we suggested a plan: They were to make their own toys from the heap of the discarded pieces. They were to put together something new, complete, and beautiful, and this was to be done in cooperation of them all.

The children were asked to contribute ideas because the toys were not simply to be repaired but to be rearranged in a new manner. They decided, for instance, to reassemble the broken dolls and their torn-up clothes so they would represent various races and nations, with an object in their hands typical of their group. The children painted, sewed, scraped, hammered, stuffed bellies, redrew faces, pasted hats, and covered animal figures with pieces of fur and wool. They drew lots to win each completed new toy, which was then presented to the lucky winner.

The hypothesis behind the experiment was based on a logotherapeutic view of human nature. The goal was to establish a meaningful connection between their toys and their lives, to arouse their interests, to let them see a value in the things around them that meant something to them, and to challenge them with a task that allowed them to use their energy constructively. The children were led away from a mere consumption of gifts and toward a goal-oriented activity that allowed them to contribute their ideas and efforts through a creative process, toward a task to be achieved.

It did not occur to any of the children to frivolously destroy the things they had so painfully assembled. The parents could not believe their eyes when they saw how carefully their children handled their new toys. Half a year later we had to discontinue the experiment with this particular group of children because they had learned to handle their toys adequately, and not enough broken toys were available.

I do not think we would have achieved the same result if we had handed the children vases to be smashed against a wall. I am convinced their aggressiveness would have become stronger and the familys' living rooms would eventually have resembled a battlefield, under the supposition that smashing was the proper way to discharge aggressiveness.

Perhaps our small-scale experiment contains a hint for parents and educators: If we want to help our young, *we must help them find tasks they consider meaningful, and let them complete these tasks.* Beyond that, we must be prepared to set an example and live our lives in a meaningful way, dominated not by the gratification of needs and the discharge of drives but by conscience, will, and reason.

When I accuse evil,
it occurs no less frequently,
but it focuses
everyone's attention on it.

And the manifold evils
people see
discourage them
in their fight for the good.

When I pay attention to the good
it doesn't occur more often,
but everyone's hope
is directed toward it.

And even the little good
people see,
strengthens them
in their fight against evil.

Elisabeth Lukas

CHAPTER 4

Youth: A Continuous Search for Meaning

Youth! What an inexhaustible subject for all generations, a wellspring of eternal longing for some, a source of continuous irritation for others, a seething force driven to create the new (with no idea what that might be) without demolishing the old and with little appreciation of what the old has accomplished.

We speak these days of change, a worldwide sense that something has changed, something to do with our young people. But has there not always been change, perhaps more gradual than today, but change that started in youthful hearts and minds? Tensions between old and young are age-old; they are as much part of the rhythm of human existence as tides in the sea. Still, there is something in the air that has never existed before—in the same air the young of our world are breathing. It contains not merely particles of chemical pollution but a "spiritual pollution" (if I may use this term), particles of a shattered whole that can no longer be put together: the treasure chest of the ethical Good. Youth today is breathing in a skeptical nihilism that results in psychological illness and this, in turn, is causing allergic overreactions—aggressiveness, destructiveness, and vindictiveness. Similar to physical allergic reactions, they may be triggered by minor causes and make living together more difficult.

Here lies the problem of the conflict between our generations. There is a "gap of silence," a noncommunication between the two sides that has one thing in common: a sense of resignation. In a lecture, Jochen Gerstenmaier, professor at the Institute for Empirical Pedagogy and Pedagogic Psychology of the University of Munich, stated: "The *only* thing parents and their children have in common is resignation."

This negative view has some justification. The neurotic conflict between the generations has increased to an extent that is almost unbearable. This is particularly true in our technological, highly developed "First World." This is more than the natural process of the young gaining independence. It is hostility carried out in various ways, not always in open confrontation, but often subtly offensive, as the two sides refuse to speak to each other.

How has it come to this? Three explanations seem especially pertinent. They deal with the question of meaning and therefore with the essence of humanness. I shall discuss how the unfulfilled quest for meaning is responsible for the general resignation, and how the fulfillment of the quest for meaning can be a healing factor in the smoldering conflicts between young and old. But first a few words about our present situation (in Middle and Northern Europe as well as in North America).

The first explanation of the existing problem is *early maturation and prolonged adolescence.* It is an observable fact that childhood today ends earlier and adulthood begins later than ever before. This means that adolescence starts sooner and lasts longer; in some cases, it does not seem to end at all. A century ago, adolescence was an appendage to childhood, a short interim period on the way to adult life. Since the mid-1960s, it has become a long, tortured phase, full of attempts to "find oneself"; these sexually mature half-children, half-adults stumble from difficulty to difficulty, wildly protesting that life demands too much.

Early maturation undoubtedly is dependent on glandular processes of the body, triggered by emotions and the stimulations of a changing lifestyle. Children receive calorie- and protein-rich food while not being required to use their energy by working; they are offered a multitude of toys without needing to be creative in play; they are exposed to the influence of the media, leaving no room for imaginative, childlike fantasy. This forces them to deal prematurely with thoughts that force them out of childhood.

Children as young as 11 years of age discuss the dangers of smoking, have had free sex education without a concurrent consideration of moral values, are bombarded with music and a cacophony of noise, know all the tricks of computer games, and revolt against the demands of life... all before they have outgrown the parental home. Viktor Frankl commented: "In this fast-moving time, one gets the impression that people who have no goal run through life as fast as possible so they won't notice their lack of goals." This observation fits these accelerated half-children who are being pushed, and push themselves, onto paths with no idea where they lead.

This is one of the dangers of early maturation: Part of the maturing process remains unfulfilled because there was not enough time for full maturation. If early maturing means faster maturing, there would be no objection, but this does not happen anywhere in nature, including in human nature. As Frankl demonstrated, the human being is a three-dimensional being of body, psyche, and spirit, and we must develop in all dimensions in order to mature in fullness. Medicine and psychology have shown that the three dimensions in a person develop in relation to one another: Physical maturity must precede that of the psyche; maturity of the psyche must precede that of the spirit. Although all three dimensions progress simultaneously, the physical development must be close to completion before the psychological can approach maturity, and the spirit can fully mature only after development of the psyche is almost completed.

Today, however, young people grow into physical maturity earlier than in the past. This initiates development of the psyche before its time, but growth is blocked because the young face experiences they cannot yet handle. Twelve-year-old children cannot emotionally deal with advanced sexual experiences, nor 13- year-olds with continual conflicts in the family. Thus, the psychic development of an early matured young person sputters like a dying motor, starts repeatedly, roars into life, and dies after a few yards.

Psychic development matures with delay or not at all, but is indispensable before the spirit can mature. This leads to prolonged adolescence and trouble because it prevents people from assuming control over their lives, planning reasonably, and mastering difficulties responsibly. It is, therefore, not a contradiction to say, with the Swiss psychologist Helmut Schulze, that although the young mature early, we live in an "age of infantilism."

The second explanation of the existing problem we might call *subculture versus family*. Gerstenmaier, mentioned earlier, has studied hundreds of young people and discovered that they increasingly take role models from their peer group rather than from their families. Peer groups have rapidly increased in importance and constitute a subculture that attracts the young. Gerstenmaier found that, in 1981, 40 percent of the young were more influenced by subculture than by family; in 1985, the figure was 55 percent, 15 percent higher. This remarkable shift has been described by some researchers as "abdication of parents as role models."

Without evaluating this trend as good or bad, two radical consequences for the intergenerational relationship are worth mentioning.

The first is the question of what function—what *meaningful* function—parents can still have. Since adolescence begins sooner and lasts longer, young people are financially dependent on parents for a relatively long time. In Western Germany, in 1950 more than 80 percent of 16- to 18-year-olds were working or serving in apprenticeships. In 1985, it was only 50 percent (30 percent fewer!); the rest were still in school. If parents have no function as role models and, because of early adolescence, no significant role in continuing to bring up their children, their only function is financial, and that is rather one-sided for harmonious coexistence. Family conflicts are often the result, which drives the young even closer to peer subcultures.

The second consequence of the importance of subcultures is the fact that, because mainly young people serve as role models, there is *very little "passing on" of experience from older and mature persons*. Therefore, the young must go through bitter experiences from which they might have been spared. Nor can the young obtain those meaningful values that previous generations, through laborious thinking and learning, have recognized as reliable and useful. The painful self-experiences of the young raise anxiety about the future, while their parents' inability to pass on anything raises *their* anxiety, and both factors lead to resignation.

Resignation prompts many parents to give children their freedom, not because they trust them but because they feel powerless. This reduces conflicts in the short run but widens the "gap of silence" between generations. It is not that parents are unwilling to talk about certain taboos, but rather that the young are saturated by discussions with their peers and don't want to talk with parents.

This strange combination of parents financing children without much communication has an ironic side effect. Since parents no longer serve as role models and children make their own decisions, parents are not even suitable scapegoats. The less influence they have, the less they can be blamed for failure. Parental abdication is a burden for the young, and they need new scapegoats, so they accuse society. This may partly explain the gigantic protest movement that goes far beyond past revolts.

The third explanation of the youth-adult problem is the *shrinking of conscience and basic trust*. In many years of family counseling I have learned much about parental love and suffering. I don't mean that parents are innocent; rather, they suffer as much from misguided children as children suffer from mistreating parents. In general, mistreatment of the child is caused by a parental conscience that is too strict and narrow, while the parents of problem children suffer from the fact that their child's conscience is undeveloped or not attended to. Parents suffer not so much because their children develop slowly, fail in school, or have physically disabilities, but because their children are insensitive, self-centered, mentally lazy, or "drop-outs" from life. In most cases, these parents have not been too strict but were trying to bring up the children by understanding their needs. This, however, can easily boomerang, because if things come easy, expectations and demands increase.

Take the car, for instance. Cars make it easy to get from place to place; at the same time, people are less inclined to walk long distances. Now there are robots that make it easier not only for our bodies but our minds, and this is critical. Autos have gadgets that warn when something is out of order—a fantastic advance that saves the driver independent thinking. But the disadvantage is that if the control system fails, the driver might drive without suitable headlights or tire pressure. Of course, people are not spoiled by techniques but by the way they use them. If the forces of the human spirit are softened by comfort, we fall victim to a weakening that keeps us from withstanding hard knocks.

In this sense, parents' fulfilling of all their children's wishes is questionable because it makes the child incapable of "doing without"—a quality that is demanded of each of us in the course of growing up. Even more problematic is the fulfillment of desires artificially created by our consumer society. Children are given expensive gifts not because they want them, but because they are heavily advertised. This is dangerous because it leads to consumption without appreciation, and to the attainment of material things without experiencing meaning.

Most of our youth have grown up in a world that did everything to make their childhood as pleasant and easy as possible, and not only in material matters. In most cases, they received love and affection and not simply a room for themselves or ten teddy bears instead of one. But what many missed are the opportunities *to give*, not only to receive. In the greenhouse atmosphere of pampering, hedonism and egoism flourish; the consequence is the withering of the organ that helps us find and interpret meaning—the conscience. Need gratification cannot take the place of meaning fulfillment that goes beyond needs and points beyond the self.

With the withering of our conscience goes the loss of basic trust. If everything is measured by our own well-being, we feel lost when it is threatened. If we have not learned to think and act responsibly, we are frightened when faced with unavoidable responsibilities. If we never learned to make sacrifices, any restriction seems life-threatening. Because everything that comes easily demands a continuation of the easy life, the "easy-liver" considers all difficulties unacceptable, a "horror."

Young individuals are caught in this horror. Facing difficulties makes them panic. They lack the trust that a difficult life can be a successful life, the insight that meaning can be found even in situations of despair and suffering. They are caught between two extremes. On the one hand, they go through experiences beyond their age level for which their peer group could not prepare them, and through which they cannot work emotionally, thus causing a block in their psychic development and creating anxiety about the future. On the other hand, they have never had experiences of persevering, doing without, and sacrificing, which would give them trust in life and in themselves.

This was a brief analysis of our present situation in the "First World." Now a word on possible *solutions*.

The current situation cannot be solved or dissolved by either the older or younger generation. But every life situation and social condition offers specific opportunities. What can and must be removed are the blocks to specific opportunities, so that change toward the positive becomes possible. This is our goal, and we must be aware of it: Aimlessness following on resignation is the biggest block.

Three goals need to be carefully considered in order to break this deadlock. Our young must rise:

a) from infantilism of the psyche to maturity of spirit,

b) from peer dependency to family friendship,

c) from need gratification to meaning fulfillment.

Everything that brings these goals closer will be helpful during a complex and extended adolescence. It is not my intention to consider what adults can do to influence young individuals to approach these goals. We have to admit that our influence today is not strong enough for that. But there are some words on the principle of hope.

Today, pessimism seems to be the only acceptable form for a realistic view of the world. (What is not pessimistic is not perceived as realistic!) This trend may be justified for some aspects of the future. The thoughtless waste of raw materials or the wanton destruction of resources justifies fear of the future. The arms race and population explosion also are reasons for serious doubts. Yet there are areas where pessimism is not warranted. These areas allow optimism in spite of everything; a true realism does not force us to be pessimistic, but requires what Frankl called a *tragic optimism*.

Viktor Frankl's (1983) keynote address at the Third World Congress in Regensburg, Germany was called "Arguments for a Tragic Optimism." He showed that the present dangerous situation demands a strength of spirit that can grow only in the soil of a fundamental, unbroken trust in meaning. As long as people hope, they behave as if hope exists, resulting in a turnabout of these conditions. It is not true that what is realistic *must* be pessimistic; rather, what is optimistic *can* become reality.

I want to apply Frankl's arguments for a tragic optimism to the young people of today—to present arguments that adults, though they have little influence on those growing up, must not lose faith in them. There is reason to hope that the young have the strength to find meaningful goals even through detours and wrong turns, and that they are lovable even when they don't act that way. This seems to be a better solution to overcome blocks than educational guidelines when education is resisted. What, then, are the arguments that will allow us to counter the resignation of youth?

The first is an undeniable argument from which other corollaries follow. Young people are *on a continuous search for meaning*. This does not mean that adults do not also search for a meaningful life. But most adults have at least partly succeeded; they have had meaningful experiences already and are nourished by what they found. The "full granaries of life's harvest" are among the joys of old age.

In contrast, young individuals have not had much chance to discover meaning structures. Their existence is full of yet-unlived possibilities. But precisely because they have not discovered many meaning potentials, their search is more urgent. If they want to fulfill innate longings for a meaningful life, they have to start the quest. To start a harvest for their empty granaries they must go out into the fields, rain or shine.

Adults can be content with half- or three-quarter-filled granaries, and rest on their achievements, experiences, and bravely-borne sufferings; the young cannot sit idly with empty granaries. This fact has motivated the human race through history and will reach into 21st century—youth devoting itself to a continuous search for meaning.

This runs counter to any justification for pessimism. Scientific proof and human experience have demonstrated that we have a reservoir of strength that under normal circumstances is not at our disposal. It becomes available as soon as we see a meaningful task. We then receive additional strength to fulfill this task. A meaningful task is like a key that opens our reservoirs of strength. To put it conversely: If we see no meaning in our actions, we lack the strength to act and so we fail. Some people believe they must first accumulate enough strength before they dare to tackle a meaningful task. They keep accumulating strength but never become strong enough because their inner reserves are not accessible without a meaningful task to live for.

Young people today have many opportunities to find urgent tasks. As soon as they become aware of them, they will quickly mature; from a near-eternal adolescence they can thus become young adults facing a world for which they can and must become responsible. It may not be a beautiful world to which they awaken, but it will end their infantilism and challenge them to a maturity of spirit beyond our imaginings.

This process has already begun. It was the young generation that first drew attention to the task of preventing pollution and ending the arms race. Their methods were not always the best but we are at the beginning. To survive, however, humanity needs new ideas and these must come from each new generation.

As stated, the first goal in bridging today's generation gap is for the young to grow from infantilism of the psyche to a maturity of spirit. The older generation can do little or nothing to promote this development. Regardless, it will take place because the young will become aware of the tremendous and urgent meaningful tasks around them, challenging their will to meaning and motivating a proportionate response.

There is another argument for a tragic optimism of the young: We are approaching our limits. Limitless demands cannot be satisfied on a limited planet, and we are close to the limits of economic growth and social welfare. Experiencing limitations has an amazing effect: *It raises the values within existing limits.* For example, individuals who carefully tend their small fenced garden plot will not be as careful in unfenced woods and meadows. There they may litter and throw away cans and other refuse of civilization. Limits warn us: "This was given to you, no more!" This makes the gift special and precious. Frankl even stresses that only the limitation of life by death gives meaning to our actions. In an unlimited lifespan, everything could be postponed and nothing would need to be done.

What is limited becomes precious if limits are recognized as such. This is also true for the family. Families have come to dangerous limitations. The high divorce rate makes children distrust marriage, but mutual-consent cohabitation and communes have demonstrated limits too. Emancipation often leads to emancipated loneliness. At the same time, a healthy, intact family, where each member has a meaningful function, has become a rarity. But rarities rise in price, not only in dealing with antiques. Thus there is hope that youth in its search for meaning and values will rediscover the value of the family. In truth, the family is much more limited than the peer group, in numbers and in scope. But precisely in its limitations the family offers irreplaceable values and a security not available elsewhere.

There is a natural law which found expression in the Fourth Commandment ["Honor your father and your mother, that your days may be long in the land..." (Ex 20:12, ESV). –Ed.] and has a psychological impact on modern men and women who have lost much of their instinctual heritage. The law states that inner peace depends on peace within the family.

This was once expressed in a counseling session with a father. His sons had rebuffed him, although by working long hours he financed their studies and entertainment. He said: "I count on my hour of death. Their innate wish for reconciliation will bring them back to me." This was his tragic optimism speaking. The ultimate reconciliation with a father and mother is an irrevocable precondition of inner peace. For this reason alone, the current silent hostility between the generations cannot be lasting. The peace sought by youth in vain in the outer world depends on peace within. When conflict and disagreements threaten, as they do increasingly, the peer group with its vague commitments will dwindle in significance, while rekindled family relations will provide support in an unstable world. If we follow this to an extreme conclusion, we may suspect that complete reconciliation between young and old, rich and poor, and among all nations will come in the death hour of humanity. Thus, the second goal in bridging the generation gap—moving away from peer dependency toward closer ties with the family—will be achieved by the young generation without the necessity for the older generation to insist or to beg for it. The role for the older generation lies in its readiness for reconciliation, to wait patiently until awareness of limitations makes possible a newfound cooperation.

There is another argument for a tragic optimism for our youth. I mentioned earlier how a greenhouse atmosphere of coddling and pampering brings about a shrinking of conscience and basic trust. Many psychologists and educators have described this but few as well as Viktor Frankl. He pointed out that an affluent society and a welfare state can satisfy all human needs except one: the innermost need to find and fulfill meaning. If this is true, then the reversal of affluence, certain to come sooner or later, will bring about changes.

As long as only *luxuries* are in short supply, people will fight for what's available but will get adjusted to the new situation. We are probably in the early stages of this development now. But when *necessities* become scarce (or what we have come to consider necessities), a painful era will begin. It will be painful for all, but especially for our children. They will have to lower their demands and expectations, and no substitutes will be at their disposal. Hysterical defiance, angry foot stomping, demonstrative refusals, secret pressure on parents, or insulting of teachers will no longer help. What will young people do then, who have never learned to do without or to make sacrifices?

In counseling the young, sometimes I feel sorry for them because they are so utterly dependent on good living conditions. During and after the Second World War, my entire childhood was overshadowed by misery; this turned into an enormous advantage, a treasure of experience that will be with me the rest of my life. I have learned to do without with no damage to my psyche and I believe this is true for most of my generation. If tomorrow I had no car, no TV, and no butter on my bread I could still be happy and content as I fulfilled my tasks. Should I lose my job I would not founder in idleness and apathy. Even under blows of fate, the loss of a loved one, I would not be driven to self-destruction.

But what will be the reaction of a generation that is disconsolate when the motorcycle breaks down or a soccer game is lost, a generation that needs several TV sets because it cannot bear to miss a program, that considers suicide when grades are poor? It is not difficult to guess. They will rebel, and when this leads nowhere, they will profoundly suffer. *Suffering will bring change.* Their continuous search for meaning will lead in a new direction. From a consumer society where the only unfulfilled need is meaning, attention will turn to nonmaterial values, because many material goods are no longer available.

Books will be read and thought about once more. The magic of soft music will cast its spell over the young, whose musical needs were satisfied by deafening mechanical noises. Virtues like goodness and faithfulness will no longer be scorned as old fashioned, as they were in our present world of moral convenience and personal devaluation. To be able to study in school and work at a job will be appreciated again—the joy of having abilities and the opportunity to use them. Young people will see meaning in particulars whereas before their whole world seemed meaningless.

It almost seems as if the young of today sense the painful path they will have to go from need gratification to meaning fulfillment, from *to have* to *to be.* Those who "drop out" voluntarily sacrifice luxuries. Religious and meditative practices have noble features. Modern sports like jogging and surfing place heavy demands on bodies softened by an easy life. Cross-country skiing and bicycling tours offer opportunities for contemplation far from crowds, even though it involves strenuous exercise. This is a welcome trend that promotes qualities such as self-control and self-restraint, and directs the young towards higher self-chosen goals.

Waiting behind this orientation toward meaning is the orientation toward one's own conscience. Conscience is that part of a human being that is least influenced by self-centered motivations, pointing at something beyond the ego, yet within our responsibility. Conscience helps us to discover what is most meaningful in a situation and how to find meaning even when it appears to be against one's own needs. The "will to meaning" is not just one "need" among others, it is *the* human attribute which makes us truly human. No animal searches for meaning. There are many languages including animal language, but the language of conscience is meant for and is heard only by humans. The "will to meaning" demonstrates our readiness to listen to the language of conscience. With this readiness comes our basic trust in life. We cannot always expect that life will gratify our needs, but we can hope and trust that life always offers a chance to find a meaning that satisfies us more thoroughly and deeply than anything else.

This brings us to the third goal in bridging today's generation gap. As stated, this goal is to move from need gratification to meaning fulfillment. Here, too, we have reason for optimism within our tragic situation. As affluence recedes, the resulting suffering will bring us to a new awakening. In the young it will liberate impulses to find new ways to reach our shrinking conscience and to regain trust in life.

In conclusion, we have no reason to despair or ultimately to doubt our children. We acknowledge that our influence has diminished, as have our opportunities to guide them to what we consider best. We admit that generations of parents have not always given the best guidance even though given this opportunity. Many mistakes have been made.

Adults bringing up the young have lost their function as role model as well as that of scapegoat. The function of "money supplier" has remained, as has something more essential: *the task to have faith in our children.* It is a faith that—even without our influence and example—they are on the right path whatever the obstacles and confusion, guided by their continuous search for meaning.

What is man?
There is no answer
because there are millions
of answers.

He is crazy
and superintelligent.

He is a beast
and a saint.

He is more primitive than an animal
and yet a spiritual being.

So what is man?
There is an answer:
A creature
that is self-creating.

Elisabeth Lukas

CHAPTER 5

"Family First": The Meaning of Love and Family

Following the traces of my honored teacher, I want to emphasize that love is not a means to pleasure for the purpose of gratifying one's needs, as Sigmund Freud once proclaimed. Love is rather an expression that transcends one's gratification of needs. It is what we call in logotherapy a *coexistential act*. According to Viktor Frankl, the human being can be seen as a unit of three dimensions: the body, the psyche and the spirit. These three dimensions correspond to three possible attitudes to love.[1]

1) *The sexual attitude*: This is the most primitive form of love, which happens when the physical attributes of a person arouse another person sexually.

2) *The erotic attitude*: This goes beyond mere sexual appeal or lust to the psyche of the partner. The person is infatuated by the partner's psychic qualities; emotions are aroused by the character features of the other. Here, too, the partner is still exchangeable by another person with similar character qualities, by a person of the same type.

3) *True love*: This presents the deepest penetration to the spiritual dimension of the partner, the relating to the other as a personal being. Frankl wrote:

> The true lover does not "care about" particular psychic or
> physical characteristics "of" the beloved person; he does not

---

1 See Frankl, V. E. (1986). "On the Meaning of Love," in *The Doctor and the Soul*, 2nd ed. New York: Vintage/Random House.

care about some traits that she "has," but about what she "is" in her uniqueness. As a unique person, she can never be replaced by any double, no matter how perfect a duplicate. But someone who is merely infatuated could probably find a double satisfactory for his purposes. His affections could be transferred without difficulty to the double. For his feelings are concerned only with the temperament the partner "has," not with the spiritual person the partner "is." (Frankl, V. E., 1986, *The Doctor and the Soul*, p. 136)

Here the difference between the concepts of Sigmund Freud and Viktor Frankl becomes apparent. Freud called "infatuation" a "blocked striving"; that is, the person was blocked from a hidden genital-sexual drive. Frankl would have agreed that it was "blocked striving," but the block would be understood differently, as blocked in the direction of true love.

Spiritual dimension	TRUE LOVE	Blocked striving according to Frankl
Psychic dimension	EROTIC ATTITUDE	
Physical dimension	SEXUAL ATTITUDE	Blocked striving according to Freud

According to Frankl, true love is not a sublimation of sexuality, as Sigmund Freud argued, but a precondition of human sexuality, which in its humanness always goes beyond a purely sexual act.

This difference in thinking is the reason why Freud defined one of his therapy goals to be that patients should regain their capacity to pleasure; Frankl modified this therapy goal to state that patients should regain their capacity to love. This does not mean that they must not become occasionally infatuated, but if there is never a deeper personal relationship, a large area of meaning fulfillment is missing in their lives.

Based on these ideas, we can observe in practice that crises in partnership commonly develop where both partners have different attitudes towards loving each other.

	SEXUAL ATTITUDE	EROTIC ATTITUDE	TRUE LOVE
TRUE LOVE	unhappy or unfulfilled relationship		optimal relationship
EROTIC ATTITUDE	danger of sexual blocks	harmless flirtation*	unhappy or unfulfilled relationship
SEXUAL ATTITUDE	insignificant sexual adventure*	danger of sexual blocks	

*no crisis

If both partners have the same attitude toward love, which is located in the table's diagonal, a good understanding of each other is possible, even in the case where both are only looking for an insignificant sexual adventure or a harmless flirtation. In the case where both are capable of true love, an optimal relationship will take place.

But if the partners have different attitudes towards love, then unhappy, unfulfilled relationships or sexual blocks will be the result. The danger of sexual blocks emerges whenever one partner seeks sex, the other emotional ties. In a traditional marriage, often the partner seeking sex is the male, the one seeking emotional ties the female. Since one of the partners cannot give what the other is looking for, there is no real tenderness, nor can there be a satisfying sexuality.

The place in the table, labeled "unhappy or unfulfilled relation" indicates that one partner loves, but not the other. "Unhappy relationship" refers to the person who is not able or does not want to return the love that is shown. This being unable or unwilling brings that individual into inner conflicts and produces unhappiness. "Unfulfilled relationship" refers to the person whose love remains unrequited.

Regardless, this person will not become unhappy, although this sounds strange. This is because, if the meaning of love is to enable us to see another human being in his or her uniqueness, as Viktor E. Frankl defines it, this seeing of the beloved person's specific values, existing and potential, is enriching, whether love is requited or not. True love must necessarily enrich the lover. Frankl wrote:

> In fact, this inner enrichment partly constitutes the meaning of his life, as we have seen in our discussion of experiential values. Therefore, love must necessarily enrich the lover. This being so, there can be no such thing as "unrequited, unhappy love"; the term is self-contradictory…. We must remember this: that infatuation makes us blind; real love enables us to see. (Frankl, *The Doctor and the Soul*, pp. 150-151)

From the definition that true love is not "blinding" but, to the contrary, enables us to see the fullness of the partner—in religious terms: as God created him or her; it follows that the partner *cannot be exchanged* and the relationship is *lasting*.

Physical characteristics pass, affection does not last, but spiritual acts remain: Love to another person survives even the partner's death! Death can destroy only the existence of a person, not the essence. The essence of a person, which is the focus of a lover, is not limited by time, as all great philosophers have told us. In a similar way, true love does not depend on the physical—on sexuality or on physical proximity, not even on the partner being alive. Of course it wants to express itself *through* body and psyche: Tenderness and sexuality are expressions of love.

Summarizing, we can say: If two partners grow beyond infatuation to true love, they are capable of fidelity (because the partner is not exchangeable) and permanence (because of the durability of their relationship). The natural consequence under normal circumstances is a proper sex life.

Let us now turn to the family and the question of how family crises can be interpreted and avoided. We know that the health of the family is the basis for the health of its members, and where the climate of the family is poisoned, the members can hardly remain well. Medical research has demonstrated that 20 percent of all illness could be avoided if the family life of the patients were intact.

But how do family discords come about? The theory that all family members always take part in family discords is wrong. In the family, too, individuals in their uniqueness are important and have the freedom and possibilities of choice about their attitudes and behavior. To explain family conflicts by looking for causes will necessarily fail, because the behavior of one member can always be explained by the behavior of others, all the way back to Adam and Eve—this is no real explanation and leads to a relinquishment of the responsibility of the individual to a "responsibility of the community," which is no real responsibility at all. By trying to uncover the interactions of family members, one easily gets stuck in the search for causes and finds only victims, but no culprits. As long as all family members sees themselves as victims of the other members, help is not possible.

Viktor Frankl, who founded a meaning-centered psychotherapy, also planted the seed for a *meaning-centered family therapy*, which judges behavior of a family member less by its causal history than by its direction toward meanings and goals. Such a meaning-centered family-therapy, for example, is also interested in why a father is aggressive, but raises the question whether it is meaningful for the family's health that he rages sometimes, and if not, whether he might not quit *for the sake of the family*, regardless of why he started and whether this reason still exists.

If causal chains are interrupted against causality for the sake of a goal, they continue in a different direction. So, for example, if the causal change has the pattern that no family member likes the father, therefore the father is aggressive, therefore no family member likes him, and so on, and if this causal chain is interrupted against causality in the way that the father suddenly is not aggressive any more *although* nobody likes him, then there is a good chance that one day he will be liked again by the other family members and the cause of his aggressiveness has vanished too.

We see that to break this unfortunate circle it is sometimes enough for *one family member* to perform a "goal-directed pro-action," which gives new meaningful direction to the chain of events. Such "goal-directed pro-actions" are intentional acts of the will, carried by nothing else but true love. They are not caused by any external events; it is possible for one person to act differently toward a new goal.

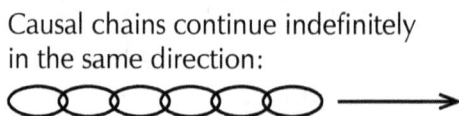

Causal chains continue indefinitely
in the same direction:

If causal chains are interrupted for the sake of a
goal, they continue in a different direction:

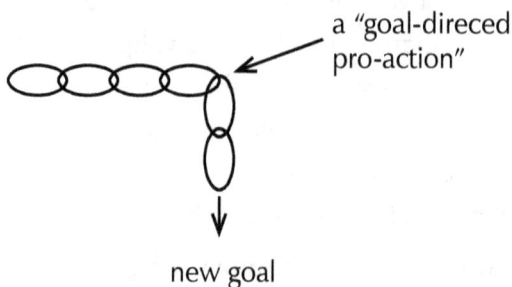

a "goal-direced
pro-action"

new goal

Sometimes I tell my patients about the comparison of the feelings with the phenomenon of an echo. If we shout something negative on a mountain, something negative comes back, so that we again shout something negative; this chain can only be broken by a "goal-oriented pro-action." There must be a decision to shout something positive for a change, in spite of the previous negative echo. In contrast to the causal concept, in this scenario not everyone is a victim but an "initiator," even if the initiative is limited to reacting in a certain way. This leaves responsibility with the individual for the benefit of the family and does not get lost in a hazy common responsibility, where no one is responsible at all.

A *meaning-centered family therapy* in a logotherapeutic sense therefore works mainly with individuals. Occasionally, several family members are counseled together to draw attention to the *whole* family to the goal of the actions of the individual member that benefits the whole family.

For working with families, *three rules* are useful, which are based on the logotherapeutic view of human nature:

1) Meaning awareness in the family is the realization that each member needs, and is needed by, another member; without this realization, the family becomes meaningless and thus unbearable.

2) Family happiness is independent of favorable outer conditions; satisfactory family life is only determined by inner attitudes to outer conditions.

3) Development in the family is not predetermined by its history; but the future of the family will partly depend on the present actions of its members.

Rule 3 indicates that "Adam and Eve" are not to blame for any present conflicts, because family history is not a *decisive* factor for the present family climate. What is decisive are the actions of every member, based on his or her inner attitude. Here each member decides the extent to which it is possible to be influenced by past actions or to be prompted to new actions.

Rule 2 indicates that the vicious circle between inner and outer conditions is not an unchangeable force. For example, the following is a false assumption: Single-parent families have poor outer conditions, causing family conflicts that, in turn, make it difficult to improve outer conditions; thus, there is no possibility to solve conflicts. This is an unacceptable oversimplification. What is far more decisive is not the fact of the single parent but his or her attitude, how the condition of separation and being alone with the responsibility of bringing up a child is handled under the given social conditions.

Finally, rule 1: The "need and being needed" within the family means that each member should have a meaningful function within the family, which must be recognized and fulfilled. This determines the happiness of each member within the family and even how bearable the family is. As soon as one member is no longer aware of having a meaningful function—where that individual feels useless or merely "used," is not ready to fulfill such a function, is apathetic or lazy, where any member of the family exhibits traits such as dominance, egocentricity, and self-importance—in each of these situations, there is a danger that the family will become "unbearable" and a crisis breaks out.

Family crises begin when the functions of family members show gaps or collisions, making a harmonious life together difficult or even impossible

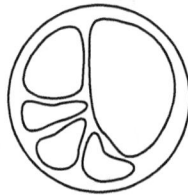

Each member has a
meaningful function
within the family

↓

Family in harmony

Functions of
family members
show gaps

Functions of
family members
show collisions

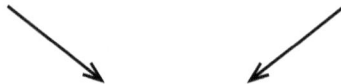

*Family in danger of
crisis*

for all family members. An example of a functional gap occurs when a parent does not take care of the children, or the grandparents are excluded.

An example of a functional collision is when parents have conflicting approaches in bringing up children, or the father and the son fight about occupational plans. I often compare the family with an orchestra, where each instrument has its unique, meaningful voice. The harmony of the music is disturbed either by an instrumentalist either failing to play at the right time (a gap) or playing at the wrong time (a collision).

Just as it is with an orchestra, the meaningful function of a family member is not always the same. It undergoes changes with time, as the children grow and mature. So we notice the following guiding principle: *A family can only live in harmony if every member has a meaningful function*, even the baby or the aging grandparent!

A last point I want to mention is *the criterion of priority*. Fulfilling the meaningful function in the family has priority over fulfillment of other meaningful tasks. This derives from the responsibility of the individual with respect to other family members. No one is forced to start a family; every adult is able and allowed to live alone. But once individuals have decided on partnership and family, they accept the obligation to fulfill the functions necessary to maintain and further this partnership or family. Although it sounds like common sense, it has to be said clearly in our times; even the adoption of a pet obliges the person to take care of it.

The quintessence of the criterion of priority is the precedence of the meaning fulfillment within the family over other such demands. In some cases, it is possible that a task is so important and meaningful to devote oneself to a matter outside the family, that the family must be neglected and a functional gap develops, but this is possible only if the other family members agree to extend their functions to close the gap. For example, if one parent wants to go abroad to further a career: When the spouse and children agree "for his or her sake," there is no big problem, the functional gap is closed. This does not mean that they will not miss or replace the parent; only that the family is not harmed and the situation is bearable for all.

Returning to our comparison with an orchestra in this situation, we can say that one missing voice is filled by other instruments to continue the orchestra's playing. It is also possible that a short-term meaning fulfillment elsewhere is in the long run beneficial for the family. Then, too, a crisis can be avoided.

For instance, a parent enters a rehabilitation facility for six months to begin recovery, and the children are placed in a children's home during this time. This indicates a short-term functional gap, which cannot easily be filled by persons who are not familiar to the children. But this is the price to pay that the parent will later be fully "functional," when physical and perhaps psychic strength is restored.

Under normal circumstances, however, a break of the criterion of priority constitutes a real danger to the family and therefore must be avoided whenever possible within a meaning-centered family therapy.

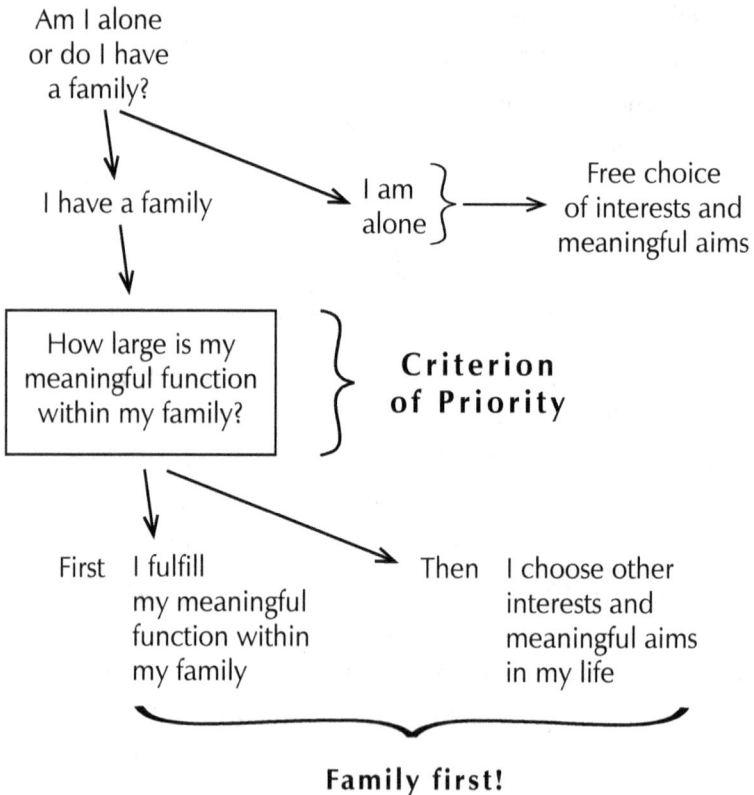

Am I alone
or do I have
a family?

I have a family → I am alone } ⟶ Free choice of interests and meaningful aims

How large is my meaningful function within my family? } **Criterion of Priority**

First I fulfill my meaningful function within my family → Then I choose other interests and meaningful aims in my life

Family first!

Doing without a break of the *criterion of priority* means growing into the dimension of "true love." True love within the family, however, enables the family members to see the other family members as they are and at the same time in their best possible form. That is the deepest or highest goal of all logotherapeutic work with families: to help them to love and to help them to see. But in order to move in this direction, the therapist and counselor must also see patients and clients as they are and also in their best possible form, in order to stimulate them in this direction.

Thus, in the final analysis, the work of the therapist is based on love, not between the two individuals, but between two human beings. Therefore let me close with a wise saying by Pestalozzi: "You must love people, if you want to change them!"

QUESTIONING FRAMEWORK FOR COUPLES COUNSELING

STEP I

A couple describes a certain conflict, which they have gone through without solution. (Counselor = C)

> C.: "What do you think was the actual element that upset your partner?"
>
> Both answer.
>
> C.: "Is that correct, what your partner has presupposed?"

If one or both fail to agree, they can correct the presumption.

STEP II

> C.: "In case a similar situation occurs again, do you see any possibility to prevent your partner from getting so upset?"
>
> Both answer.
>
> C.: "Would this change of behavior, which your partner mentioned, really help you in similar critical situations?"

If one or both fail to agree, they can describe what instead would help them, but they are not allowed to make greater demands.

STEP III

C.: "Are you ready to realize the possibility which you mentioned and to change your behavior in a similar situation, independently of what your partner does?"

Both say "yes" or "no."

If only one says "yes," this can be enough to increase hope for the family.

C.: "Are you happy about the readiness of your partner to change a little bit? Can you accept it as genuine?"

No further discussions; session is ended.[1]

---

1   For an expansion of these ideas, followed by examples of this exercise, see Chapter 9 on page 89.

"I cannot"—that's readily said,
so quickly and easily,
it hardly requires a thought,
only a motion of the tongue.
And a possibility is dead.

How would it have been,
if it had remained alive?

Would it have made
the unexpected expected,
the unbelievable believable,
the desired available?
Would it have become part
of the meanings of the world
and become reality of
what was waiting to become reality?

"I cannot"—that's readily said,
but look, I also can question the "I cannot,"
it hardly requires much energy,
only the will to overcome.
And a possibility is born.

How would it be
if it remained alive?

Would it change the unchangeable,
unlock the locked,
awaken the sleeping?
Could it bring back
the difficult, the uncomfortable
but—seen within the meaning context
of the world—immensely blissful
"Yes, I can"?

Elisabeth Lukas

CHAPTER 6

Love and Work
in Frankl's View of Human Nature

Notwithstanding the existing variety of psychological schools, there are at present only two complete concepts of the human being that have been proposed in the field of psychology. One school was founded by Sigmund Freud and was tacitly taken up by nearly all subsequent schools, including the very differently structured school of behaviorism. The other was founded by Viktor E. Frankl. The future may belong to the latter. That the birthplace for both concepts was the Austrian capital Vienna is a peculiar coincidence. One could, however, also see it as a logical and necessary development. It first started with ingenious discoveries based on trial and error and a continuous process of self-correction which led via the "aha-effect" to a realistic scientific theory. Be that as it may, we can't reconcile both concepts of the human being, the "old" and the "new." To the extent that they appear to be thesis and antithesis, so they are incapable of synthesis. Therefore, for the time being, every practicing psychologist has the prerogative of choosing the preferred concept. But once the choice is made, the healer can act, research, and interpret only in terms of the chosen system in order to remain loyal it.

As the two great aims in life, *work* and *love*, are inevitably interconnected with the fundamental conceptions of human life, I would like to compare and contrast these two concepts to bring out a specific and unmistakable distinguishing characteristic. It can best be circumscribed by the concepts *monad* and *self-transcendence* or simply with *closedness* or *openness* of the each individual to the world.

Traditional psychological theories, whether because they have their source in psychoanalytic thinking or because they are based on considerations of learning theories, all regard the human being as a *monad*. This means for them that the person is a closed system. Within that system, there are a number of movements and processes, forces of drive and will, emotions and cognitions, conditionings and automatisms, creativity and spontaneity, consciousness and unconsciousness, influences from within and without, and reactions to them in a plethora of patterns.

There was much theorizing about the different layers of the "I" and about maturation and its different phases, which either stabilize the system or upset its balance and cause psychological disturbances. Much research was conducted about the strength of needs and the question of their satisfaction, which contributes considerably to maintaining normal functioning of the closed system "the person," while stress, shocks, and frustrations endanger it.

Seen from such a perspective, normality is equal to inner balance (homeostasis), and psychological stability is defined as an intact monad. According to this interpretation, whoever is able to release his drives in an acceptable manner, to realize his needs and desires adequately, to not repress his hurts, to adapt his conditioning mechanisms to demands, and to find his identity, is regarded as "healthy."

But where the monad is disturbed because drives are suppressed and irrational maladaptive behavior is enforced by unconscious complexes, external psychological trauma inhibit the unfolding of the I, or where faulty conditioning curtails self-confidence, the natural desire for happiness, success, and attention can no longer be satisfied; psychological stability falls into neurosis or psychopathology. We see that the closedness of this concept of the person lies in the fundamental egocentricity of the system; reduced to a simple formula, such an individual says: "Good is what is good *for me,*" or "I stay healthy if I get what is good *for me,*" and "I get sick if I don't get what is good *for me.*"

Should we want to talk about the phenomenon of work, we cannot make an exception, and within this specific psychological approach must define "work" as "good work" if it is good *for me*. That would mean it is not boring, is not too stressful, does not impose excessive demands, brings enough rewards and recognition, and leaves ample freedom. Should we want to talk about *love*, we cannot make an exception either. It would also have to be judged positive insofar as it offers advantages for an I, such as human closeness, a partner for talking openly, as well as for security, safety, and the satisfaction of drives and pleasures.

I don't deny that in the concept of the monad interactions with the environment are possible, for something has to be invested in work or in a partnership or there could be no return benefits. But this interrelationship is also governed by the principal doctrine of optimal wish satisfaction of the person concerned, just as every human action and feeling in general, from its deepest motivational roots, is oriented towards the satisfaction of one's own needs and the maintenance of an internal balance. It is a concept of the person that appears very clear and reasonable, yet leaves a certain uneasiness when it tries to answer an age-old question about the essential identity of the human as a "being chasing after happiness"; specifically, "one's own happiness."

The fundamentally different approach, which was developed by Viktor Frankl, starts from the premise that the person is not a monad and not a closed system. According to Frankl, the human being, unlike other creatures we know, has an opening to the world. In his concept, the many different energy potentials found in the monad model are by no means denied, as they demonstrably exist. They are, however, complemented and elevated by a motivational force that cannot be placed on the same level with needs and processes of the psyche, because it reaches beyond the self, "transcending" the self into the environment. It is *the will to meaning*.

Of course, forces of will are already present in the traditional concept of the person in psychology, but what is special in the concept of a "will to meaning" that destroys any idea of a monad, is the repeatedly highlighted fact that this meaning is not centered on the self. It is much rather the *specific meaning of a situation,* which contains an objective component that is to be grasped subjectively. Meaning, therefore, is the link between a person and the world and is never merely "meaning for me" but always simultaneously a part of "meaning as such." The answer to the question about the human being is thus no longer that the individual is a being chasing after happiness, more specifically personal happiness, but that the person is *a being on a search for meaning, specifically for a meaning in the world.*

Let us examine this enlarged concept of the person with the examples of love and work. Taking the human ability for self-transcendence into account, "good work" is then equal to "meaningful work," and "meaningful work," in turn, refers to work that brings something meaningful into the world or that changes something that exists into something better. In short, it brings something good closer to perfection. Normally this kind of meaningful work is rewarding even more so than work that is merely not overdemanding or performed merely in exchange for money. There may, however, be extreme situations in life in which meaningful work is extremely difficult and very troublesome. Thus the reward it brings is not short-term happiness but is nevertheless valuable and important and therefore endured with fortitude. The criterion of self-interest is valid only within the limits of the monad. Beyond it, the meaning of the moment as such is valid.

It is no different in regard to the phenomenon of love. According to Frankl's thinking, love is much more than the satisfaction of an elementary or sublimated sex drive. It involves an element of meaning belonging to the external world, namely, to the loved one. Just as the value of the object to be created merges with any work that is worthy of human effort, so a love worthy of the human being merges with the worth of the partner to be loved, on whose well-being the attention of the lover is concentrated. And again, committing oneself to another normally reflects into one's own heart, but there may be situations in life when it is difficult either to maintain a close interpersonal relationship or to let go of it, depending on what the meaning of the situation demands. Where this is achieved, it is out of a genuine love; it is a love that enables a person to disregard his or her own self-interests.

THE CHILD IN THE CIRCLE

A beautiful example of the confrontation of both psychological schools is provided by Berthold Brecht in his drama *The Caucasian Chalk Circle* in which he describes two women who fight for the same child. One of the women is the natural mother of the child who, without doubt, would be entitled to the child. The other woman, however, raised the child under great hardships and loves it as her own. The functioning of a monad can now be explained from the behavior of the natural mother. Her rights are supposedly being curtailed and, as a result, her feeling of self-worth is upset. In order to regain balance she must insist on enforcing her rights. The judge, having placed the child in the center of the chalked circle and the women to the right and left of it, commented that the true mother would be able to draw her child to her. She pulls with all her might. The servant who raised the child on the other hand, mobilizes her ability for self-transcendence and lets go because she reasons: "Before the child in the middle of the circle is torn apart, I'll waive my claim to it!" In the drama the judge then finds it easy to decide which woman has the real claim to the child.

For the psychologically trained observer, it is not difficult to predict which of the two women would have been happier if the judge had decided in terms of his original statement: the natural mother with her triumph over her rival to the detriment of the child, or the servant with her painful sacrifice for the love of the child. We can safely assume that inner contentment would have been found with the latter even if her feeling of self-worth had decreased much more than that of her counterpart.

Although the story is an extreme example, it demonstrates unmistakably what is meant by a person's being open to the world. The biological mother does not open up; she remains closed. She has to work through the trauma of losing her child, she has to abreact her aggression against her rival and has to defend her interests. She is busy re-establishing her own psychological balance and being so busy with herself and her problems she is hardly aware of her environment. She does not really see her child although she fights for it. She does not really fight for the child but much more for her own happiness. She is the prototype for a *being chasing after happiness*.

The maidservant, on the other hand, opens up to the world. She also has a trauma, for she gave up her boyfriend for the child. She also has aggressions inside her about the mother who once indifferently left the child and now comes and demands it back. Indeed, her psychological balance is at least as much disturbed—and her interests to be defended are at least as strong—as those of the biological mother. In spite of her own problems, she is able to take cognizance of her surroundings, and what she sees in them is an innocent child on whom pain is to be inflicted. It is a senseless suffering and this is where her will to meaning revolts and gives her strength to leave her monad and, with it, to leave all her problems. An objective meaning of the situation becomes recognizable: The health of the child must be maintained! And the woman hastens to fulfill this by transcending herself. She acts as is appropriate for a *being in search for meaning*.

If we share the idea that the human being can see into the surroundings by means of spiritual perceptions and find meanings there that are not directly connected to emotional needs, then we have to re-admit two concepts into psychology that had previously been disposed of—the concepts of *freedom* and *responsibility*.

In a closed system, neither can exist, because there the mainly unconscious forces of drives and experiential history determine the actions of the present, and where we have predetermination and predestination we don't have guilt. In an open system, it becomes more complicated. Impulses from the external world with their attributes of "meaningful" or "meaningless" meet with the existential longing of the person for a meaningful life and challenge spiritual forces that are neither open to predetermination nor predestination. They are free forces whose application or lack of application must be correspondingly justified. Let us contemplate this with an example that has less to do with love but more with work.

THE REPORTER OF THE DEVIL

There was once an impressive film titled *The Reporter of the Devil*. This film was supposed to have been based on a true story about a miner who was buring in a mine and had to be rescued. According to experts, there were two alternatives for rescue. One was relatively quick—direct drilling; the other would take somewhat longer—constructing a tunnel. After estimating the available oxygen and the condition of the person in the hole, it was assumed that he would be able to survive either rescue operation. That is, he would survive the longer lasting rescue operation as well as the shorter. But, naturally, all the estimates were more or less guesses as communication with the victim was difficult.

The accident attracted many curious onlookers, among them a reporter well known for his excellent news coverage. He used all his influence to encourage the construction of the tunnel, the prolonged rescue operation, thus gaining enough time to offer exciting stories to his readers and fill his column for days. Many strangers descended on the place from all over to witness the rescue; because they required board and lodging, they brought additional income to the village. When the miner was finally reached, he was dead.

This story shows us in the person of the reporter someone who does excellent work and is crowned with success. He writes exciting reports and earns publicity and reward. Yet everyone will have to agree that, in this case, he went too far: A human life was at stake, which should have taken precedence over any reporting, however good it may be. In psychological terms, we can again choose from two alternatives. One comes from the monad model and the other allows for self-transcendence. In the monad model there is, as we stated, no guilt. The action of the reporter can be perfectly explained as an expression of his personality. One might perhaps suspect an inferiority complex resulting from his childhood, which demands as compensation his reaching the summit of his career. Or one could plead for a deficiency in social sensitivity, which can be traced back to lack of social training in his development. Some would place at least part of the responsibility on the conditions of the social environment that supports the egotistical plan of the reporter and the considerable pressure that was exerted on him by his readers.

In Frankl's concept of the person, all these arguments are only partially valid; they represent only one side of the scales, namely, the fluctuations of the reporter's psyche. On the other side of the scales rests the meaning of the situation, which entails saving the accident victim. We must distinguish very carefully between an external psychological influence, such as the social pressure of the environment, and the presence of an objective meaning, which has no influence as such but is only discernible by the individual's spiritual perception. The situation of the trapped miner and the meaning of his rescue, which lies encoded in it, are exclusively environmental elements, even if they have a certain intrinsic demand character. They have nothing at all to do with the psychological stability and coping capacity of the reporter.

Until now, there has been agreement in thinking but now we reach the assertion that separates the new concept of the human being from the old one. It is the contention that, because of his ability for self-transcendence, the human is almost so independent of his psychological stability or coping capacity as to give a spiritual response to meanings that he perceives in his environment by fulfilling them or not. This is a person's responsible freedom which has been introduced into psychology by Frankl. *It is a freedom for fulfilling meaningful tasks in spite of diverse (inhibiting?) influencing factors.* Self-transcendence is thus also a "being able to overcome oneself," a "being able to react beyond the limits of the monad" into a world full of meaning, even if that meaning is only vaguely perceived. The conscience, by definition, is the human sense organ for detecting the specific meaning of a situation; and the freedom to respond to this perception is *responsibility*. Guilt can be described as resulting from a "No" to the question of meaning, the "No" that was expressed by the reporter in the film.

CHALLENGES

The second example also concerned an out-of-the-ordinary event that probably does not belong to everyday life. Yet we will find numerous similar challenges in every ordinary life if we search for them, although most would not have the same serious consequences. What is interesting is that they concern mainly the phenomena of love and work. There are mothers who want to extract top achievements from their children in order to bask in the reflected glory and pride. There are also mothers who want their children to have the best possible education so as to give them a good start in life. The fine distinction is in the self-transcendence of the latter. There are women who complain about frigidity because their men don't manage to help them achieve optimal orgasmic experience, and there are women who can give themselves tenderly to their husbands, even if sexuality does not mean that much to them. Again, self-transcendence makes the fine difference. Whoever really loves another person, whether a child or a partner, can't chase only after his or her own happiness and misuse the other as a means for satisfying selfish desires.

This is analogous to work. There are authors who write books in order to reach the best seller list and there are others who write to bestow a gift on their readers. There are doctors who want to build up a profitable business and others who want to fight disease. There are assembly line workers who do piecework to achieve a higher living standard; there are others who support their large families with their work. The fine difference lies every time in self-transcendence, namely, including objective meanings from the environment in one's own motivation.

For me as a psychologist, these reflections do not hinge on moral considerations but rather on the psychological interpretation of the human being. Can a person incorporate the welfare of others or the meaning of a work to be created into one's personal decision-making process? Sigmund Freud said "No"; Viktor Frankl said "Yes." This "Yes" is not an antithesis, nor a simple negation of the no, but no less than a new definition of the person. As Frankl asserted: "The more he forgets himself in his task and gives himself to his partner, the more he is human and becomes himself."[10]

Thus happiness, which is held by all the other schools to be the highest aim of human striving, was for Frankl no aim at all. For him, happiness is the automatic by-product of a meaning-filled existence, which in Bernanos' words draws its contentment from "the grace to be able to forget self."[11]

Having clarified the positions of both concepts of the human being, I would like to add two short reports from my psychological experience to round off the subject. They are associated with Frankl's perspective of love and work and may give food for thought to the professional and the layman.

A CASE OF SPIDER PHOBIA

The first case is of *diagnostic* interest and relates to spider phobia. A young girl went into all sorts of fits of screaming and unconsciousness when she saw a spider anywhere. The history of her affliction indicated that there had been a number of events in her childhood which could have had a precipitating character, especially the fact that as a young child she had lived in a dilapidated old house. There had been many spiders that often had even crawled into her bed. Another factor was that her parents had often sent her to bed during the day as punishment, which made her very unhappy. Whatever the reason, the parents later moved to a better house. The punishments ceased but the fear of spiders remained and was intensified to such an extent that even the picture of a spider in an illustrated book could start a phobic attack.

Because I not only search for a dominant problem and its genesis while investigating the history of an affliction but on principle look simultaneously for positive attending circumstances, I asked the girl whether she had ever had an experience with spiders that by any chance had been a positive one. To my amazement she answered in the affirmative. Only once in her life had she managed to pick up a small spider from a window sill with her handkerchief and throw it outside without breaking into a panic, storming out of the room or screaming for help. Naturally, I was very interested to hear how about a person who had loathed spiders since childhood but could never touch them, who later developed a full-blown phobia, suddenly managed to throw a spider out of the window without any apparent trouble. What could have happened?

The reader can imagine that some trace of self-transcendence had to be involved, otherwise the monad would not have opened. A dear friend of the girl had been visiting and was not feeling particularly well. She had just been discharged from hospital and was still feeling very weak and had therefore gone to rest in the girl's bedroom. They chatted and then the friend fell asleep. The girl rose and stood at the window and there saw the spider. She was confronted with the choice of either running from the room screaming, and thereby waking and frightening her friend, or removing the spider quietly. She chose the latter course. Her consideration for the friend was stronger than the power of fear.

I think we should learn something about psychological diagnosis from this example: A person can't just be pigeonholed in a set of typical behavior patterns. Anyone can at any time react atypically if he or she has a strong enough reason for it. Therefore, it is risky for a diagnostic inquiry to collect exclusively negative connections that exist between the past and the present of a person because this could create the impression that the present is inescapably dependent on events of the past, which is simply not true. Sometimes a little bit of love—love in the widest sense— is enough to give new and unexpected impulses to the present.

A CASE OF OBESITY

The second story, which I consider even more remarkable, is interesting from a *therapeutic* perspective. It concerns a case of compulsive snacking and eating, that is, excessive consumption of food. The case has a tragic component because it concerns a man who, due to a handicap in his lower limbs, was confined to a wheelchair and, for that reason, naturally moved very little. This, together with his symptoms and the resulting overweight condition, had consequences that were detrimental to his health. He suffered terrible constipation, stomach cramps, etc., which did not react even to strong laxatives.

His overweight had long since been diagnosed by medical doctors as psychological and soon the hypothesis of satisfaction replacement was held, which of course fits without exception any handicapped person because he always has much to give up. However, every therapy approach based on this theory had failed, and when the man came to me for consultations he had hardly any hope of improvement.

To be honest, I also saw little opportunity for reducing his dependency but I had my eye on something else. Although the man already had to bear the heavy burden of his handicap and additionally the unpleasant digestive problems which could not easily be corrected, some part of his life had to be worth living.

Therefore, I did an *existential analysis* with him in the best Frankl tradition to discover where his various interests, talents, and abilities were to be found. Perhaps these could then be emphasized to bring content, engagement, and meaning into his rather uninteresting and inhibited life. During our talks, it became apparent that during the war the man had spent several years in a prisoner-of-war camp, and because of his own bitter experiences had a deep sympathy for the fate of all innocent prisoners throughout the world. He could get very upset over news of torture or inhumane prisons and emphasized again and again how he would like to do something for these poor, tortured people.

I don't even recall who first thought about the organization Amnesty International, but it was inevitable that our talks should get to it at some time and suddenly the man perceived a meaning offering itself to him. An organization like Amnesty International could be supported from the wheelchair. He telephoned, made contacts, established a branch of the local agency in his apartment, catalogued articles, and wrote newsletters to members of the organization. In short, he became a forceful voluntary helper of Amnesty International, and after some time he became the hub of many important links. Several weeks later, I sent him a note but heard nothing from him. Occasionally I invited the man for further therapeutic talks but he did not return. He was too busy. Somehow I considered this positive, for I had the feeling that the meaning which suddenly enriched his life was more important and salubrious than any, even the best, psychotherapy.

Nevertheless, I was surprised when, several months later, the man appeared at my consulting rooms without an appointment. By chance, he had been in our area and wanted to tell me about the many interesting things he was doing. He started telling me about them in detail but I could hardly concentrate on his words. I simply had to stare at him in amazement the whole time. He was slimmer than I had ever seen him.

"How did you lose your excess weight?" I inquired.

He laughed. "I don't know myself" he answered, "but I do know one thing: When Amnesty International needs me, I totally forget eating!"

How can this history of an affliction be interpreted psychologically? Can we, in terms of the monad system, accept without hesitation that the patient only changed his type of satisfaction replacement and that now he finds satisfaction in meaningful tasks in this worldwide organization instead of as before with food? Is this perhaps compensation for what he missed during childhood? I think we would be unfair, not only to the man but also to the value of his new task, if we were to declare his involvement as an expression of a neurosis and his help to political prisoners as a means for working through his psychological complexes. Every human contribution, however small, if it improves or beautifies something in our world, contains an objective meaning, reaching far beyond the subjective level of complexes and compensations.

It is, therefore, no disgrace to admit that meaningful work can make our therapeutic work actually superfluous; whenever a meaning experience becomes concrete, so much self-transcendence is activated that a neurosis no longer has a chance. At any rate, we psychotherapists could be as necessary as before to guide our patients towards a meaning experience. And that is exactly the function that Viktor Frankl formulated for his students, to look beyond every psychologically ill patient for a "being in search of meaning" who not only needs help facing psychological disturbances but also for exclusively human suffering. Love and work may be very strong vehicles for emotions of interpsychological processes and they may have all their sources in drives and motivations, but they are aimed at the environment in which human existence wants to find meaningful fulfillment. And only to the degree to which that is achieved is *Being* really human.

A game must be played
for the sake of playing,
and not winning.

A deed must be done
for the sake of the deed,
and not of the reward.

People must be loved
for their own sake,
and not for
releasing a drive.

A life must be lived
for the sake of living,
and not for the pleasure
it may bring.

Elisabeth Lukas

From a Wrong Idea to the Desert Storm: A Logotherapeutic Approach to Conflict Resolution

Much has been said about the Gulf War that shook the world at the beginning of this year [1991]. It is not my intention to talk about the Gulf War; politics are not my forte. My concern is with an idea, to be specific, with *the central idea* of logotherapy around which all its statements revolve.

This central idea contradicts any notion of war as a safeguard for peace. Or to formulate it differently, the Gulf War was based on an idea too, but on another one, which, when it is examined from the perspective of the central idea of logotherapy, appears to be extremely questionable.

As is well known, Viktor Frankl conceived the human being in the light of spiritual freedom. This spiritual freedom is neither a physical nor a psychological entity, but rather an extrapsychological entity, and as such inaccessible to mere psychological tools. Therefore it seemed to be lost for a long time. Those who used the methods of logotherapy were the first to reopen the blocked access to the freedom of the human spirit for human sciences such as psychology and psychotherapy.

To demonstrate the full implications of Frankl's work, let us use a simple model:

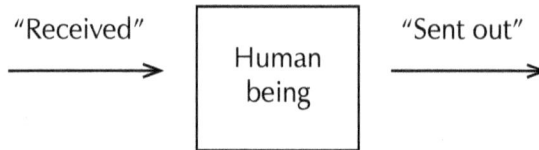

"Received"   [Human being]   "Sent out"

The rectangle in the middle represents the human being, who is at the center of our considerations. From the left, an input arrives; this arrow stands for everything the human being receives from the world throughout his or her lifetime.

Examples of the left arrow include received love and hate, received attention and indifference, received chances and handicaps for development in life. The left arrow defines the boundaries within which living growth is possible, a large or small area. Who would, regarding these areas, dare to talk of justice? They are not fairly distributed, nor are the gifts that everyone receives from the world. They are not even fairly distributed for newborns or the unborn in their mother's wombs. There are always some who receive more and others who receive less.

On the right side of the model is an arrow that goes out from the human being. It represents everything the human being puts forth and sends into the world.

Examples include all love given and hatred spread, attention shown and indifference demonstrated, opportunities granted to one person and obstructions wished on another. The right arrow defines the boundaries within which the development of the outside is influenced by a human being constructively or destructively. Referring to these areas, there is no equality either. Everyone produces different effects.

The "lines of contact" between the human being and the world are therefore the one where the left arrow impacts, and the one where the right arrow starts. Two lines, which can both be marked by a letter: on the left with an "E" for "experience"—because everything received is somehow "experienced" by the person, and on the right with a "D" for "decision"— because everything sent out has to be "decided" more or less consciously.

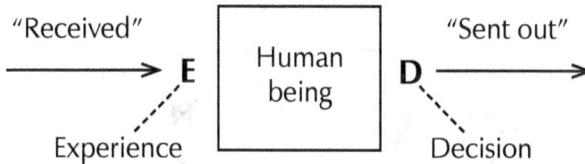

Let us now examine the relationship between the left and the right arrow, between what is received and what is sent out. Is there a relationship? Perhaps a causal relationship? Is what will be given automatically determined by what is received? Is perhaps the "D," which the person is supposed to decide, only an illusion, because actually the experienced "E" "decides" the power and direction of the right arrow?

As we shall see, this is not only a question of the existence of human freedom of will as such, but at the same time the question of the existence of *an autonomous being*, of a human "I" that cannot be derived from anything else. If the "received" and the "sent out" had to be absolutely the same quality, that is, if the right arrow depended entirely on the left one, then no genuine, true "I" would exist, no characteristic filling of the rectangle "human being." There would be nothing but a "transit station" in which experience was transformed into something merely apparently decided, or in other words, where that which was previously received from the world was handed back to it.

This is exactly the result we reach with exclusively psychobehavioral means in human sciences research. The person who imitates role models. The person who cannot love unless already loved. The person who, if irritated, starts hitting others; who, if abused as a child, abuses his or her children; who, because trust has never been experienced, doesn't trust himself or a neighbor. A man who, because something was wrong with his mother, secretly resents women. Or a person who was oppressed earlier in life, and now enjoys oppressing the weak. We could continue these examples ad infinitum (they are the subject of innumerable novels) but the essence remains the same: What was received and experienced determines what will be sent and given out; the input determines the output, and the "D" on the right is imperceptibly faded out.

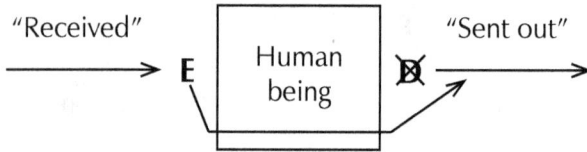

"Received" $\longrightarrow$ E | Human being | $\boxtimes$ $\longrightarrow$ "Sent out"

One may have noticed that the examples mentioned before were all negative ones. The reason is that the question of why the human being behaves inappropriately or simply does something evil is much more explosive than the question of why a person lives decently. Therefore, the negative scenarios stimulate many more attempts at explanation.

Depth psychology, in particular, has tried for decades to explain inappropriate and pathological lifestyles from their causes and seeks such causes unequivocally and exclusively in the area of "negative reception." In principle, however, it is immaterial whether we look at good or evil behavior and its hypothetical causes.

The real problem with this view of the human being is the *automatic reaction pattern*, where, alongside the "D" of free decision, all personal responsibility (the opportunity to become guilty or to gain merit) vanishes.

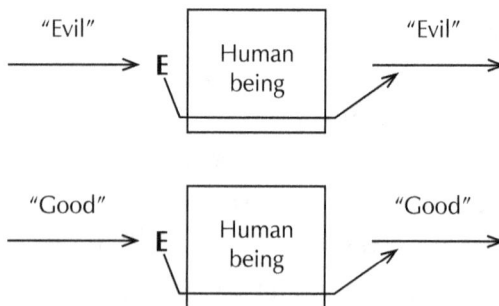

"Evil" $\longrightarrow$ E | Human being | $\longrightarrow$ "Evil"

"Good" $\longrightarrow$ E | Human being | $\longrightarrow$ "Good"

The human being as a "transit station"

In this viewpoint, evil is nothing but the automatic reaction to experienced evil; good is nothing but the automatic reaction to experienced good. Thus, evil does not imply personal culpability, nor does good imply personal achievement. The person decides nothing; he or she only passes on what is received (in old or new form).

We all feel uneasy when we consider the above statements, but research with purely psychological means cannot lead to a more differentiated version. The psyche is, exactly like the soma, "imprinted matter" and the imprint is always made by the left arrow. For this reason, behavior therapy, the great adversary of depth psychology, has adopted the same basic pattern for its original theory of conditioning: The quality of an input determines the quality of a human output, and between the two is a so-called "black box," which is an empty box, indeed.

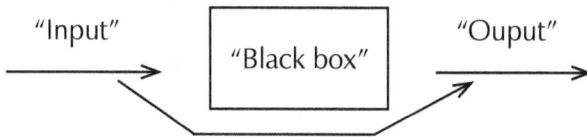

"Input"   "Black box"   "Ouput"

One has to give credit to modern behavior therapy for having taken important steps in its development. However, the analogy in the basic pattern to the otherwise almost diametrically opposed depth psychology shows that, in their undeniably valuable scientific research of the human psyche, both schools reach the same result: Human beings are "receivers" and the received matter totally determines and stamps them.

Let us, at this point, consult logotherapy. Let us fill the "transit station"— the black box—with the human spirit, and thus with freedom and creativity. From what place do spirituality, freedom, and creativity come to the person? Nothing like that could ever be found in the smaller or larger area for growth, which is allotted to every human being by his or her heritage and environment. Yet freedom and creativity exist in us. Not only do we intuitively feel it at the bottom of our hearts, it can without doubt be detected in our activities.

Seen from a phenomenological perspective, what the human being sends into the world is by no means merely a reflection of what has been received, as postulated by psychological theories, but is, in most cases, something totally different, unexpected, and new. But where does this "other," this "unique," this "new" come from? Could it be that we touch on a mystery here, one that this reveals the limits of our human sciences?

Viktor Frankl spoke of a *dimensional extension* of the view of the human being, which is required to describe the personal and existential aspects and to make them accessible to verbal formulation. In addition to soma and psyche there is a third dimension, namely the spiritual or *noëtic*, which cannot be derived from the left arrow in our model. It represents an additional arrow which reaches the person from a transcendental level and "breathes" freedom and creativity into him or her.

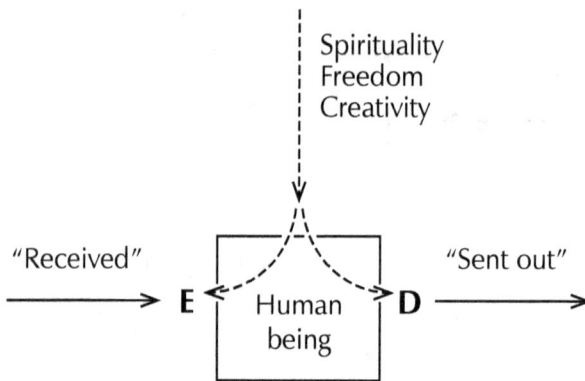

Spirituality
Freedom
Creativity

"Received"   "Sent out"

E   Human being   D

Because of this spiritual dimension, logotherapy's basic premise emerges. The person is more than just a "receiver"; it is possible to take a stand towards anything that has been received. Each individual can work at it, change it, reject it, or preserve it. And ultimately it is a decision that must be made, a choice of what is given to others. The person is really a "sender" and here and now sends something that has never before been into the world. The "D" on the right side appears again, like a spiritual finger that spans the bow and releases the arrow. The right arrow, which does not have to be like the left one, is the arrow of one's own choice, chosen from one's own quiver; it may even have been substituted for the arrow which arrived from the left.

Such a dimensional extension of the view of the human being is, when brought to its logical conclusion, revolutionary. The whole picture of the imprinted human being begins to crumble. If a person is spiritually capable of reacting differently to every experience, whether positive or negative, then neither kind of experience has any determining power. Evil, then, need not inevitably produce evil and good need not necessarily produce good. If the automatic process is eliminated, the invididual regains responsibility for all that is sent out, provided that he or she is not immature or limited by severe illness or disability. Any good or evil that is done is once again to that person's credit or discredit, regardless of what joy or pain that may have beeen received before.

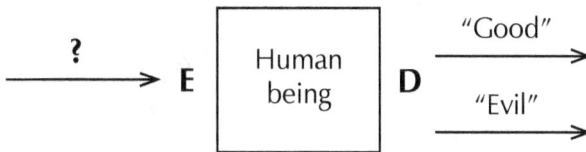

```
                                          "Good"
    ?              +------------+        --------->
  ------->   E     |   Human    |   D
                   |   being    |         "Evil"
                   +------------+        --------->
```

Admittedly, a voluntary change of quality, an "exchange," is sometimes difficult. But just as it is possible that someone can inflict abuse, even though raised with much love and gentleness, so it can happen that someone forgives graciously, even in the presence of deep hurt. In this sense, it becomes obvious why the giving of love is on a higher level than merely reciprocating it. Though it is not automatic that something positive evokes a positive response, it is relatively easy. On the other hand, offering something positive without any outside precondition or advance is a genuine decision for good, which is not supported by any example, but stands for the person on his or her own.

In this context, it also becomes plausible that a sacrifice made for the sake of someone or something doesn't have to come from faintheartedness, for instance, fear of a superior, lack of commitment, or the inability to defend oneself. It may come from an inner greatness, which is willing to make sacrifices in the service of a meaningful task.

Let us once again return to the question of the "imprinting" of the person. If the input cannot determine a person (as a noëtic being), what else has the power to do so? Logotherapy's answer is as simple as it is amazing: *The human being determines him- or herself.* This is done by the output sent into the world; the signals set, each a monument of one's own identity. The evil-doer becomes an evil person. He or she who does good becomes a good person. Those who make war are warriors, and those who make peace are peaceful. What emanates from the person, the arrow on the right, which carries his decision into reality, determines at the same time inescapably what becomes of that person. *Each life can be of a different quality than that which is passively experienced in it, but no life can be different from that which is actively decided in it!*

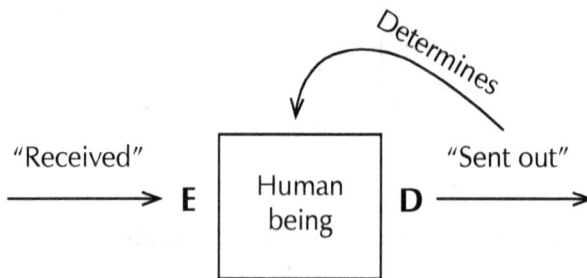

If a woman loves her husband, *she* is a loving woman. If a woman hates her husband, *she* is hateful. It is always her identity—and not his—which is formed by what she sends out, love or hate. If, on the other hand, the woman is loved by her husband, that does not say anything about her identity. She can value his love or disregard it; the decision is hers. Nor, if she is hated by her husband, does this determine anything about her identity. It is still undecided what kind of person she will become. Only if she retaliates or seeks a reconciliatory talk, only then will it be revealed what kind of woman she is. Whatever we receive can be a painful burden to us. That is, however, all it can be, if it comes to the worst. But what we give, what we send into the world returns like a boomerang with a fateful power and determines our being.

For this reason the often posed question: "I or the other?" must be declared redundant. Nobody emerges unscathed from the conflict: "I or the other?" Because if I harm someone in order to protect myself or my interests, then the stigma of having harmed someone will burden my soul and be from that point forward an indelible part of my identity. By harming others, I harm myself. And if I don't harm the other, I may endanger my own safety and advantages. Therefore, the conflict has to be resolved in a revised question, namely in the question: "What helps both of us?"

The decision that honors the best for both partners is the only one that is really good for me, because it combines personal advantages with the determining effect of a positive action. Therefore we have, each one of us, *a double motive to do good*—for the opponent, who is the primary recipient of good, and for ourselves, as we imprint ourselves secondarily in a good way.

Let us now consider the importance of logotherapy's dimensional expansion of the view of the human being for practical psychotherapy. We stated that if we do not permit a noëtic, spiritual dimension of man, which is the dimension of freedom and creativity, we have to proceed from a human psyche, which is dependent on whatever it has received. What would in consequence be more logical than scrutinizing this apparently imprinting input with the greatest care and analyzing it methodically for that purpose?

But not all received inputs need to be analyzed in order to illuminate the genesis of perverse, psychologically deviant, and repressed behavior. It is enough to look at negative input alone, because in terms of the "transit station," like produces like, and therefore only something negative can have produced something negative.

Another aspect that can also be disregarded is the objective historical truth concerning received input. The psychological reflection of the patient's subjective feelings seems to be sufficient. If, for instance, a patient has the feeling that his mother favored his elder brother, then this can be interpreted as a sufficient negative input to explain his neurotic disturbance; another possibility is that the mother may have loved both boys equally, but had to work much more with the elder, due to learning difficulties, which was the cause for the younger one's jealousy.

All this makes understandable the aims of psychoanalysis or depth-psychology, which are of the opinion that the view of the human being does not require a spiritual dimension. They aim at investigating and uncovering the patient's *subjectively negative experiences and input*, which they call "traumatic."

The logotherapist, who not only allows a spiritual dimension but even defines it as the specifically human dimension, has a totally different approach. Naturally, the logotherapist also wants to find out what shapes the person, but the deciding factor regarding whether a life will be a success or a failure is, according to its extended view, that which goes out from the person, the originator of that which is sent into the world. Therefore, the logotherapist's aim is to investigate the whole realm of free decision making and, specifically, to explore potential positive outputs, those which are meaningful.

But meaningful from whose perspective? From the patient's or the therapist's? From neither: In a patient-therapist talk, they search together for something *objectively meaningful*, which in the patient's present situation is within reach and ought to be grasped and transformed into action, from the double motive to do good: to effect positive change in the world and to heal the patient in doing so.

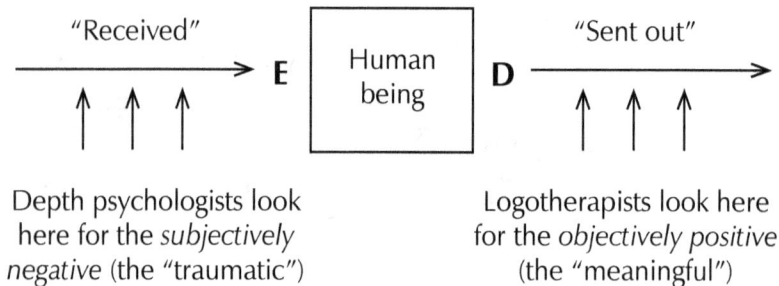

One last question remains: What is the basis for a logotherapist's optimism that even a psychologically deformed and degraded person whose past shows many traumatic intrusions, whether conscious or not, can fulfill a present meaning in life that has a bearing on the future? Let us remember the description of the mystery of human spirituality. It was outlined with the concepts "freedom" and "creativity." Creation... what is that?

Isn't that the right arrow by itself? Isn't that the entirely new, not springing from anything that came before? Isn't that the being from nothing, the underivable first, the "prima causa," the beginning of something that did not exist before this beginning? If only a spark of this creativity is present in invididuals, then we can be certain that, if need be, they can send out what they have never received, and that they can decide on something meaningful, even if they have experienced only meaninglessness. Then we can believe that each person was born to be both a "sender" and a "receiver." In the latter aspect, the person is united with all living creatures on this earth, but in the former with the Creator alone.

So much for the central idea of logotherapy. Let us now turn to the problem of conflicts and the search for conflict resolution with special reference to the tragedy that ensues, if one is attacked by another.

From the presentation of the central idea of logotherapy we see that no action of our own can be justified by actions of others. For instance, applied aggression is by no means the logical, unavoidable, and absolutely necessary reaction to received aggression, but rather a decision by someone, which also could have been very different and for which he himself is responsible. There is no law for the dynamics of aggression progression.

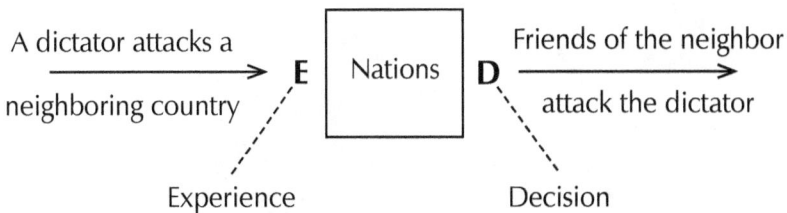

From the central idea it follows furthermore that any applied aggression imprints the initiator as an aggressor. The innocence of the victim is lost in the moment, when he, on his part, approves of aggression. The call for peace loses credibility if attempts are made to enforce it with war. Everyone who attacks is an attacker. It is impossible to attack without becoming an attacker, for whatever reason the attack took place.

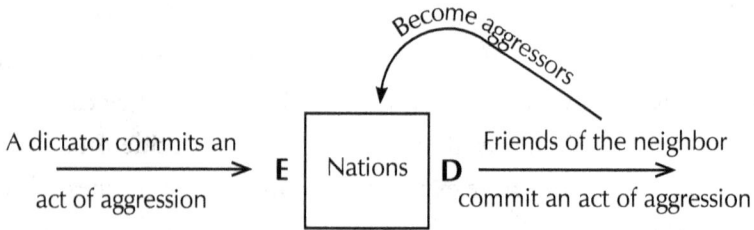

If the message of others is: "I abhor and condemn terror and the violation of human rights," it is a good message. But if this message is presented together with terror and the violation of human rights, then its content is rewritten with a blood-stained pen and now reads: "I regard terror and violation of human rights as acceptable and legitimate however, not if *you* commit them but only if *I* commit them, and only if *I* commit them *after you*, because then *you* will be guilty of *my* actions."

This is no longer a good message, since it is based on a wrong way of thinking. As logotherapy has demonstrated, a "You" can never be blamed for the actions of an "I"; the "I" is always the origin of its own actions. Whoever wants to transmit the message: "I abhor terror and the violation of human rights," must act accordingly. There is no other alternative that keeps this message credible and genuine.

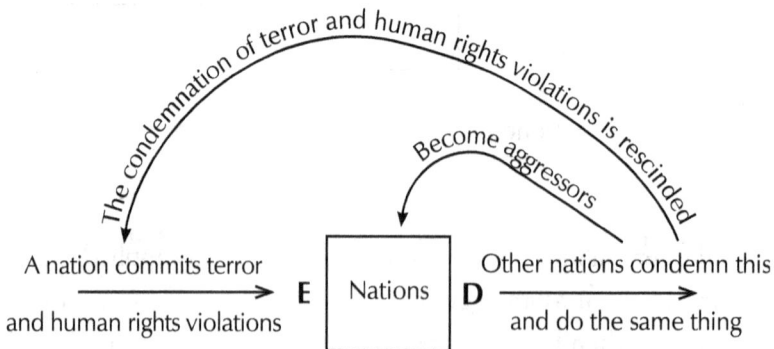

How right was Frankl when he emphasized that the end does not justify the means, but rather that bad means desecrate even the best ends.[1] No meaningful goal can be attained by using meaningless tools; one cannot reach meaning by moving away from it.

This is also true for every "holy war" or "war in the name of justice." Actually, this lesson should have been learned at the time of the Crusades and witch hunts. Evil in the name of good is and remains a paradox.

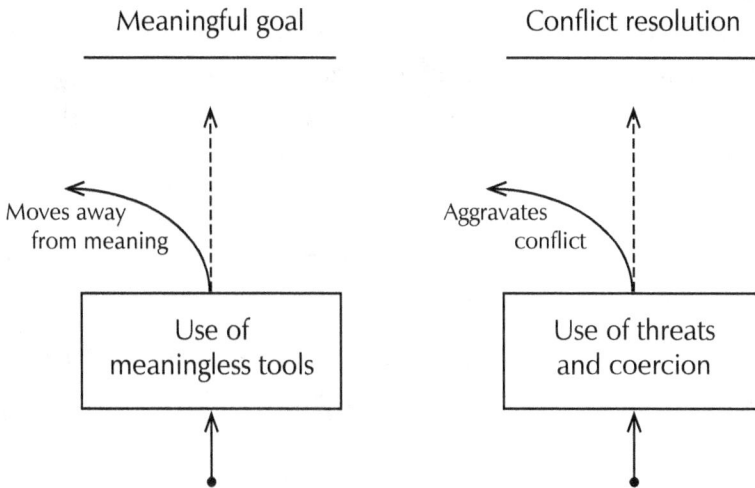

Meaningful goal	Conflict resolution
Moves away from meaning	Aggravates conflict
Use of meaningless tools	Use of threats and coercion

Let us follow this up by considering whether we can deduce guidelines for meaningful conflict solution from the central idea of logotherapy, and whether conflict solution can be contemplated within the context of a decision for good, even when evil was experienced; that is, if the "E" on the left is not identical with the "D" on the right side of the model. What is a conflict?

A conflict is a trap, and usually, in fact, a double trap. To explain the trap mechanism a simple example will suffice, although interpersonal conflicts in families and nations are far more complicated in their structure. Yet the principle is always the same.

---

1   Frankl, V. E. (1990). *Der leidende Mensch* (New ed.). Munich: Piper, p. 310.

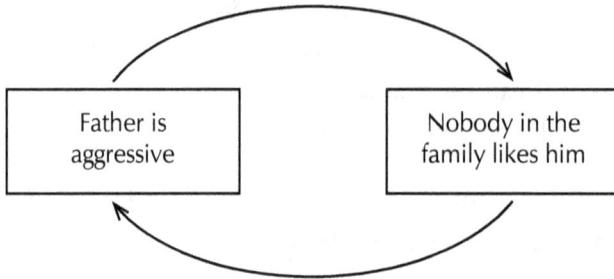

A father is aggressive, because nobody in the family likes him. Nobody in the family likes him, because he is aggressive. Traps of this nature are innumerable. A woman neglects herself, because her husband shows no interest in her. Her husband shows no interest in her, because she neglects herself.

"A" does nothing, because "B" does everything. "B" is inclined to do everything, because "A" does nothing.

Mother keeps nagging her grown-up children, because they rarely come home. The grown-up children hardly ever come home, because their mother continues nagging.

The personnel do not take pride in their work, because their boss never praises them. The boss never praises his staff, because they don't take pride in their work.

The trap could still be "exploded" if the participants did not fall into a second one, which unfortunately often happens. Only the second trap puts an end to hope.

But what is this second trap? It is a wrong way of thinking, and it will sound familiar in terms of what we said before. It is the idea that one could give back only what has already been received. It is the fatal notion that one has to remain in line with the inputs received. This is what it looks like:

Father says: "I wouldn't be so aggressive, if the family were nice and friendly to me!" The other family members say:" We would be nice and friendly to our father, if he were not so aggressive!"

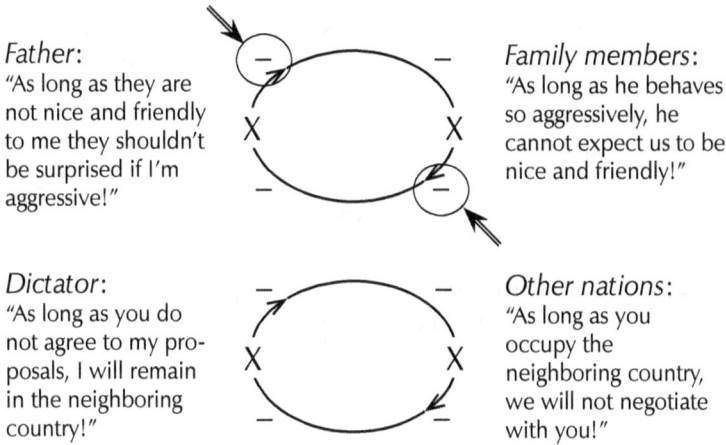

Father:
"As long as they are not nice and friendly to me they shouldn't be surprised if I'm aggressive!"

Family members:
"As long as he behaves so aggressively, he cannot expect us to be nice and friendly!"

Dictator:
"As long as you do not agree to my proposals, I will remain in the neighboring country!"

Other nations:
"As long as you occupy the neighboring country, we will not negotiate with you!"

What is happening in this situation? Each side waits for the other to take the first step. But why is everyone waiting? Because they believe they cannot send a positive arrow from their quivers until they first receive a positive one. As long as no positive arrow arrives, none is sent. The double trap is now perfect; based on this wrong assumption, no positive arrow will ever fly again and a "desert storm" can break out.

It is worthwhile examining this simple model closely. The critical points, the lock of the trap, are the minus signs coming from both sides. If only one side would answer a received minus with a sent plus, if only one side would abandon the quality of input and would independently and responsibly consider the quality of its output, the trap could open. Were both sides, regardless of received negative inputs, to decide on a positive output, the trap would dissolve into nothing.

This is logotherapy's plea—and its goal—in logotherapeutic talks with help-seeking patients; for example, in meaning-centered family therapy. Each side works out a "final advance contribution," final in the sense that it is oriented towards a meaningful end, one that aims at harmonizing the family. Effective logotherapeutic practice motivates the participants to grant and persevere with this "final advance contribution." It is also possible to talk about an "advance in loving," for true love is always unconditional and not subject to any specific achievement of the recipient.

Father:
"I surrender my
aggressiveness out of love
for my family, regardless of
how they treat me."

Father   X
+
−

Family members:
"We want to encounter
our father with more for-
bearance and friendliness,
even if he has an explosive
temper."

Family
members   X
+
−

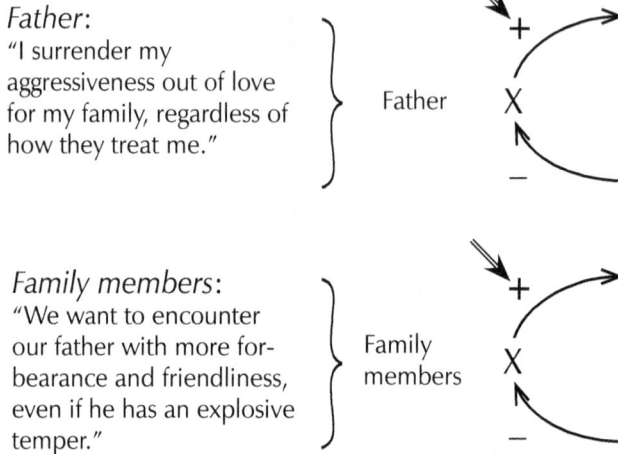

As mentioned, if only one side overcomes its own resistance to offer a final advance contribution, the entire trap can burst open. At least the hope for it to happen is increased, because the arrow that reaches the other side now is a positive one. This may gradually encourage a willingness there to send positive signals too. Goodness stimulates goodness; evil has never stimulated goodness. But even if the other side does not respond and remains negative, the psychological chain reaction is interrupted. One link of the chain has maintained its dignity, and that means that the entire chain of reciprocal degradation has become fragile. It will not bear further links of misfortune. Who would not be reminded here of Frankl's words, stating: "The physical chain reaction of the atomic bomb would not have taken place, if a psychological chain reaction had not preceded it."[1]

Only from a principle—which holds that the human being (enabled by the dimension of the human spirit) is born as receiver *and* sender and, therefore, is able to give what has never been received—can the concept of "final advance contribution" or "advance in loving" originate. Depth psychology, with its fixation on input (and on the subjectively experienced minus within the input) is, in an anthropological sense, miles away from this concept. Behavior therapy, in spite of its laudable improvements, is

---

1   Frankl, V. E. (1990). *Der leidende Mensch* (New ed.) Munich: Piper, p. 315

conceptually still on the level of reward and punishment. Let us consider: What is the precondition for reward and punishment? It is that, in case of a conflict, the opposing side always acts *first* and is then treated accordingly!

"Dear father, if you are peaceful, we will turn to you. If you shout, we will turn away!" "Dear family, if you turn to me, I will stop shouting. But if you ignore me, I will be aggressive!" The old tune: First you give me a plus, then I will reward you with a plus. But, as long as you give me a minus, I will punish you with a minus too. It is a very old song. Unfortunately in world politics we heard it fairly recently. It went like this: "If you don't withdraw from your neighboring country, I will punish you with the death of a hundred thousand...."

In the central idea of logotherapy, reward and punishment are obsolete. Sweets and a whip are used to tame animals, not humans. Individuals can spiritually progress to the understanding that the good they do is its own reward, reward for themselves, and that the evil they do is its own punishment, punishment for themselves. Human beings can recognize that everything coming from themselves forms their own identity, indeed, that a unique self cannot be achieved by taking something *from the world*, but rather by putting something *into it*. "Everyone is his own heaven or his own hell, respectively," stated Frankl.[1]

The logotherapeutic concept of the "final advance contribution" or "advance in loving" does not produce grand victories but is, in a special way, suitable for alleviating and solving conflicts of all kinds.

What exactly does it state? It does not claim that aggression, terror and the violation of human rights have to be tolerated, but maintains that, defending oneself, one should not and may not stoop to that level. Peaceful resistance, continued negotiations while keeping an outstretched hand, small concessions wherever possible, regard for the one who has been ostracized as a result of his actions, *that* would have been the "desert calm." Resolute help for the oppressed without destroying the oppressor would have humiliated the oppressor more than threatening him with destruction.

---

1   Frankl, V. E. (1991). *Der Wille zum Sinn*, (new ed.). Munich: Piper. p. 54.

I am aware that there is a great fear that oppressors and aggressors increasingly seize more power if one does not stop them in time. This fear is justified only from a short-term perspective. In the long run, greed for power and domination always reaches its limitations.

What is not intrinsically good will not prevail. It may be that a small amount of fear and suffering has to be endured before the time for renewal is ripe.

I don't think that wounds and losses can be avoided completely, but conflict resolution does not mean avoiding wounds and losses at any price, but much rather safeguarding human dignity and innocence in a situation in which everyone can easily incur guilt towards everyone. Conflict resolution means continuing to love while making it impossible for the opponent to wipe out this love with his hatred.

Many people argue that former dictators would never have become so powerful if they had been opposed from the beginning. But in no historical case do we really know how such early interventions would have looked. The fights might have been shorter in some cases, but perhaps also more violent.

In contrast to these speculations, some remarkable examples are known of nations that were attacked and occupied but renounced armed resistance. In every case, the dictators extended their realm. But what then? Permanent occupation forces are needed for the subjugation of foreign countries and tremendous pressure is necessary to annex culturally different people.

What type of government succeeds in imposing a common will on millions of oppressed people over long periods of time? How can such an enforced conglomeration of a state function economically and politically? It disintegrates spontaneously, often with the demise of the dictator. It disintegrates, as did the overextended Roman Empire in ancient times, which aimed at ruling all the Mediterranean countries, or like the huge Communist empire of our time. What is not intrinsically good cannot prevail.

In his recently published autobiography, the Nobel Peace Prize laureate, His Holiness the Dalai Lama, formulated the following credo, in view of the Chinese occupation of his country that has lasted more than 40 years and cost more than a million Tibetan lives:

> Chairman Mao once said that political power comes from the barrel of a gun. That is only partly true. The power of guns is transitory. In the end, man's longing for truth, justice, freedom and democracy will triumph. Whatever governments do, in the end humanity always reasserts itself.[1]

What a credo within the framework of a Buddhist life-style and what agreement with the "tragic optimism" in logotherapy! What harmony with the Chassidic wisdom of Martin Buber as well, who once prophesied: "Only if man has established peace within himself, will he be able to establish it in the rest of the world."[2]

Let us give a final reason for the "tragic optimism" in our conflict-solving approach. The most meaningful interaction with hostile opponents—as I would like to define it—is one that makes it easier for them to transmit positive signals. But what makes that easier? Is it whether we transmit positive or negative signals towards them? This is an interesting question.

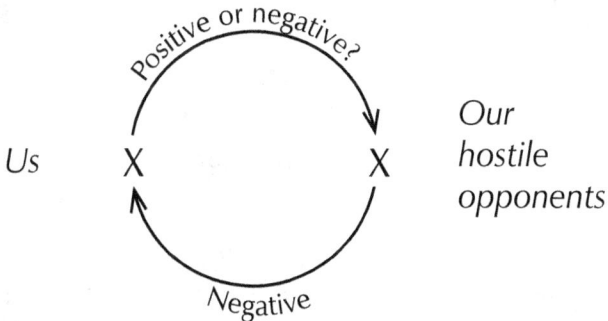

If we send something positive to them, then the negative, which they inflict on us, is not punished. Indeed, one might mistakenly assume that it is rewarded. This is the traditional viewpoint.

---

1   Lama, D. (1990). *Das Buch der Freiheit: die Autobiographie des Friedensnobelpreisträgers*. Bergisch Gladbach.

2   Buber, M. (1974). *Weltfrieden und Seelenfrieden: Erzahlungen der Chassidim*. Frankfurt: Main.

But there is also a very different one. If we send something negative, the negative signal will arrive at our opponent, who will deduce from this the "right" to continue sending negatives. If, on the other hand, we send something positive, our opponent will receive something positive; this will create a *dissonance* that one could call a "*dissonance of conscience.*" As we know, it is difficult to alternate the quality of input and output and therefore it is difficult to answer in the negative, if one has received something positive. This is difficult for the simple reason that it goes against the essence of the human spirit, which is of transcendent origin.

I once heard the story of a priest, who on his way home through the forest was waylaid by a young criminal. The robber poised his knife to strike and shouted sarcastically: "Say your last prayer, Father!" The priest replied quietly: "Yes, my son. I will pray for you." He knelt and bent his head. When he looked up again the young villain had vanished. It is not easy to stab someone in the back who is busy praying for you.

Therfore, if we send positive signals, we do not punish our enemies, but we make it difficult for them to remain our enemies. That means we make it easier for them to decide on something positive, which helps them—and us as well. It helps them, because it improves their own identity, and us, because we escape their enmity. *That is meaning.* Meaning is that which is good *for all concerned.* It can never be good for only one of the participants. Meaning is, as Frankl repeatedly emphasized, a trans-subjective entity.

If, however, we send out a negative signal, perhaps even believing ourselves justified because the enemy has also sent a negative message, then we actually lose the right to expect anything but negative reactions from our opponent. Indeed, we virtually pin the opponent down to his or her enmity. We certainly punish our opponent in so doing, but the actual tragedy of a "desert storm" is that we also punish ourselves. We, both the other and we, depart from meaning.

When, at the beginning of this year, the Gulf War broke out, many people in Europe and America went onto the streets with banners bearing slogans like: "No blood for oil." These people were wrong. No blood was spilled for oil. The blood was flowing for an idea. But it was a wrong idea. It was the notion that aggression can be banned from the world by aggression. It was the idea that suffering can be reduced in the world by temporarily increased suffering. The truth is quite different. Marie von Ebner-Eschenbach, a renowned Austrian author of the last century, summarized it in one sentence. The truth is:

"You can only have peace, if you give it."

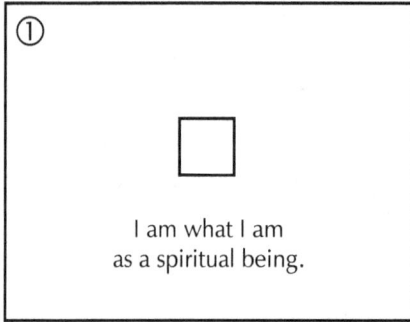

① I am what I am
as a spiritual being.

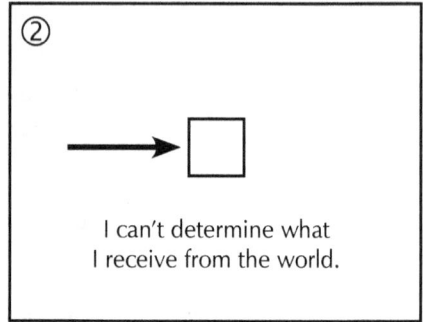

② I can't determine what
I receive from the world.

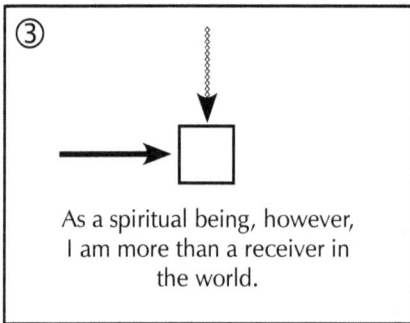

③ As a spiritual being, however,
I am more than a receiver in
the world.

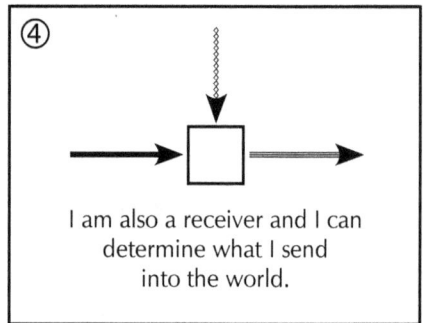

④ I am also a receiver and I can
determine what I send
into the world.

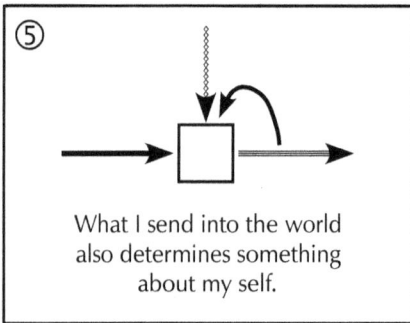

⑤ What I send into the world
also determines something
about my self.

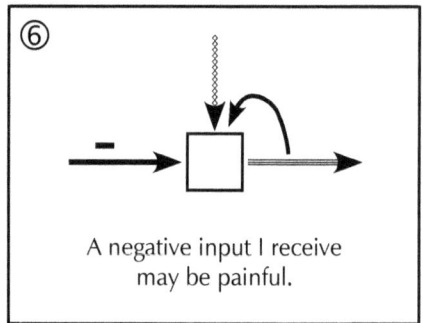

⑥ A negative input I receive
may be painful.

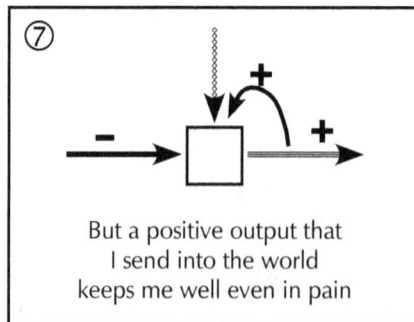

⑦ But a positive output that
I send into the world
keeps me well even in pain

I thank you, my friend.
You attacked me
and with that you gave me
strength to awaken my forgiving.

You wanted to belittle me
and the effect was
that I learned to raise myself
to my full height.

You wanted to hurt me
and with that you taught me
to endure pain
bravely and in dignity.

I thank you, my friend.
You wanted to destroy me
and with that you showed me
the indestructible within me.

Elisabeth Lukas

CHAPTER 8

Meaning-centered Family Counseling

HOW LOGOTHERAPY WORKS

L ogotherapy is a meaning-oriented psychotherapy. Its basic idea is that meaning fulfillment in life is the best protection against emotional instability and the best guarantee for psychological health.

Meaning is trans-subjective; we cannot decide arbitrarily what is meaningful to us in a given situation. We can only discover the meaning inherent in a situation. We are like archeologists studying hieroglyphs, deciphering, decoding, discovering. Logotherapy is a *dis*covering, not an *un*covering psychotherapy.

The best means for this discovery is our *conscience*, whose antenna is directed toward meaning, just as a Geiger counter is directed toward radiation. Logotherapy tries to strengthen personal conscience (which is not identical with the superego or traditional morality) and to motivate people to listen to, and to follow, this inner, intuitive voice.

In therapy, the patient wants to reach a state of health, but there is an obstacle (depression, fear, psychosomatic illness, and others). Traditional psychotherapy focuses on the obstacle, tries to understand its causes, and reduce it to size. Logotherapy focuses on a meaningful goal (logos) beyond the obstacle, and motivates the patient to jump over it in pursuit of meaningful goals.

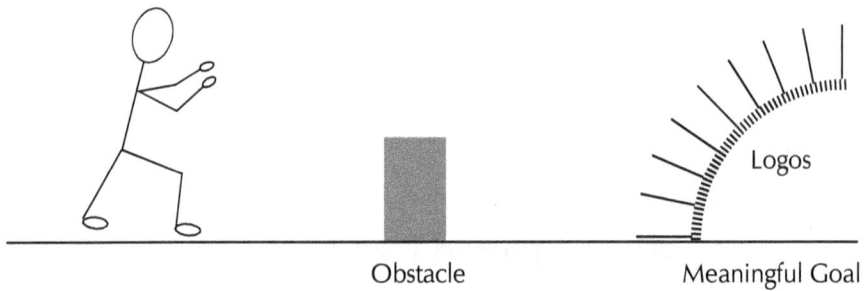

Obstacle   Meaningful Goal

• *Let's look at the jump* (overcoming the obstacle to reach a meaningful goal): Patients face the obstacle like a person standing on a diving board afraid to jump. Such people have three choices: They can wait until the fear goes away—this is hopeless; they can climb down, capitulate, and flee—this results in illness; or they can jump in spite of their fear, using the defiant power of the human spirit, and get well.

When they choose to jump, they do not receive an immediate reward and relief. Instead, exactly what is feared happens: They go down to the bottom of the water. Only then do they experience something wonderful; they are buoyed up again! They are lifted up, the water is carrying them. The jump has freed them to become healthy.

The same often happens in life: We decide to do something meaningful despite obstacles of fear, pessimism, despair, or anger. We jump over the obstacles to reach a goal or, to change the metaphor, we enter a tunnel until we see light again. We go through addiction, anxiety neuroses, suffering, family crises. But in the end, the light burns brighter than ever before.

• *Let's look at the aim of the jump* (the "what for"): Not every aim is meaningful. A jump from firm ground into the unknown can be fatal. We have to read the signs; we cannot determine meaningful aims arbitrarily. In family crises, a meaningful goal is not what is to the advantage of one member, but instead what serves the whole family. The meaningful goal for each member is what decreases suffering and increases hope for the entire family.

• *Let's look at the human being*: Within systemic family therapy the individual is seen as a function of the system. Within logotherapy, the individual is seen as a unique person who acts, not merely reacts or acts out. The person is free to act, even if a certain way of acting is difficult or not pleasurable. The action can be chosen willingly; what cannot be chosen willingly is the meaningfulness of the action. The family member is able to decide whether to jump or not. If the family system is dysfunctional (unhealthy models, reinforcement of not jumping, no assistance), the jump is difficult... but the person still has the freedom to dare it.

Logotherapy's message to the human being is twofold:

It shows the freedom to act, which exists under all circumstances	It helps to find the meaningful goal of a certain action
The "**I could**"	The "**I should**"

The "I could" and the "I should" add up to the person's responsibility to act in a meaningful way. Logotherapy, in this manner, strengthens the person's voice of the conscience.

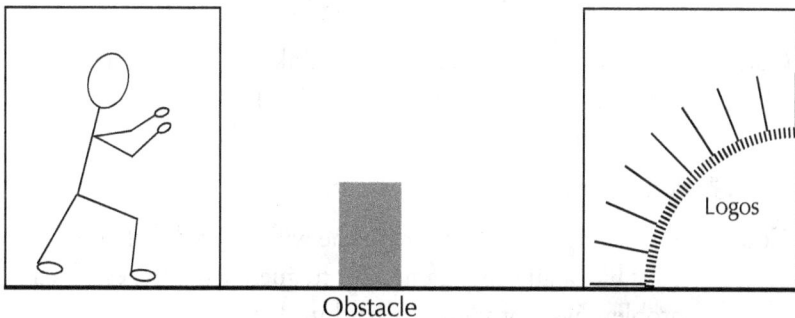

Obstacle

You are free to jump, despite all obstacles, fears, difficulties	This meaningful goal needs your jump, is calling you, is important

Logotherapists prevent individuals from brooding about obstacles by helping them to dereflect from their difficulties while showing them their inner power and abilities. Simultaneously, logotherapists show them the importance and necessity of devoting their energy to something valuable in the world.

| The [hidden] ability of the subject [the patient] | ⟷ | The [hidden] value of something trans-subjective [the Logos] |

This produces an arc of tension between the individual and the logos (meaning), and this tension serves as additional motivation to jump into meaningful actions (go through the tunnel and arrive in the light).

MODEL FOR COUPLES COUNSELING

A couple describes a conflict situation they have gone through without solution. Both partners are sad or angry about the event, and deeply hurt.

In this example, the couple[1] had a serious quarrel one evening last week and have not spoken to each other since.

Step I

Counselor [to the husband]: "What do you think was the actual element that upset your wife? What bothered her, what made her sad?"

Husband: "I think she didn't like me coming home later than she had expected. She hates waiting for me."

Counselor [to the wife]: "What do you think was the actual element that upset your husband? What made him so angry, what hurt him in his innermost being?"

Wife: "I don't know. He suddenly shouted at me."

Counselor, insisting on an answer [to the wife]: "Look, what we do is like a guessing game. Try to guess what the essential problem was for your husband in this conflict."

Wife: "During the quarrel I said that he was never punctual and reliable, not even when he was young, and that something was wrong with his character. Perhaps this offended him because he once did a silly thing in his early days and doesn't want to be reminded of it again and again."

---

1   The basic framework for this exercise is found on page 47. It is important to note that the structure is flexible and may be used with either partner, regardless of sex and/or sexual orientation. –Ed.

Counselor asks a check-in question [to both]: "Is it correct what
      your partner presupposed? Did he or she guess the element
      of your pain?"

If one or both fail to agree, they can correct the presumption, which is
an important piece of information for the other. In this example, the man
agrees but the woman does not.

She says: "My problem was not really that my husband came home
      later than promised. I understand that he sometimes
      cannot stop his work and leave it unfinished for the next
      day. What upsets me is the way he comes home. When
      he is tired, it is like I am not even there. He doesn't notice
      me. He mumbles a short greeting and hides in his room. I
      am a nobody to him,"

After correction, or if both agree, Step II is initiated.

Step II

Counselor [to the husband]: "In a similar situation, do you see any
      possibility to prevent your wife from getting so upset? Can
      you imagine a small change in your behavior that would
      help your wife endure the situation better?"

Husband: "Well, before going to my room I could sit down with
      her for a few minutes and explain why I was late and what
      has gone on in the office."

Counselor [to the wife]: "Do you see any possibility to prevent your
      husband from becoming so upset in a similar situation?
      Do you have any idea what, if you change, would make it
      easier for him to get through the situation without such
      strong negative emotions?"

Wife: "The only thing I can do is to let the past be the past and to
      avoid accusations about former times. If I blame him, it
      should be for present reasons without connections to old
      stories and his faults of yesteryears."

Counselor [Checking in with both]: "Would the change of behavior
      your partner mentioned really alleviate your conflict and

bring relief to you? Would it, indeed, help you in similar critical situations?"

If one or both fail to agree. they can describe what instead would help them, but they are not allowed to make more demands.

The wife may say: "For me, it's not so important that my husband explains, with a lot of excuses, why he is late. A little sign of tenderness. a kiss of the cheek after arriving at home, would be enough." [This is a true correction.]

The husband might reply: "She should not only let my past be in the past but also not attack my parents for bringing me up badly." [These are greater demands.]

Counselor [Stopping the husband]: "We are speaking now about the possibility of your wife no longer bringing up your past problems. The question was: 'If she would stop doing it, would this be a relief for you in a present crisis?'"

Husband: "Of course it would."

After correction, or if both agree, Step III is initiated.

Step III

Counselor [to the husband]: "Are you ready to actualize the possibility you mentioned (or have recognized in our dialogue) and change your behavior in a similar situation? Are you ready to do this regardless of what your wife does, whether she changes or not, whether she thanks you for it or not? Are you ready to do this for the sake of your family? To do it as a contribution to increase hope in your family?"

The man can say "yes" or "no."

Example of a "yes" reply: "All right, if it means so much to her, I will try to be more attentive and tender after coming home, even if I am tired and my thoughts are still at the office. She is, after all, my wife and deserve my affection."

Counselor: "And if she brings up stories of the past again, will you then give up your tenderness and attention, or stick with your new line?"

Husband: "That's difficult to say, but I shall try to keep my word. This is no business deal; it's my marriage that is in danger. Yes, I will try."

Counselor [to the wife]: "Are you also ready to undertake what you offered? Are you also prepared to try in the future what would make life easier for your husband?"

The woman can say "yes" or "no."

Example of a "yes" reply: "Deep in my heart, I have known for a long time that nothing is gained by dragging up old mistakes again and again. I do it only when I am angry. Okay, I won't do it in the future, even when I am angry."

Counselor [to wife]: "And in case you are very angry because you feel you're being ignored by your husband, will you then punish him by falling back onto your old habit, or will you stick to your new ways?"

Woman: "I don't want to promise anything but I will try my best. I don't want it to be my fault if our home breaks up."

If both say "no" during Step III, the couples counseling has to be given up because there no longer exists a true willingness to save the partnership. But in my many years of practicing this type of meaning-oriented family counseling, this has never happened. It is unlikely that two persons who seek the help of a professional to restore their marriage will refuse every possibility of cooperation. Normally, at this point both agree in some way. And if only one says "yes," this may suffice as an impulse toward a healing evolution of the partnership.

Counselor [checking in with both]: "Are you happy about the readiness of your partner to change a little bit? Can you accept the change as genuine, can you trust in this readiness? Are you prepared to be surprised positively by your partner's change in behavior without having to demand it?"

If one of the partners has problems with answering the check-in question, the counselor should not discuss these problems but just respect them and repeat the importance of the fact that every change of the self can be realized without preconditions, whether the partner believes in it or not or whether the partner reinforces the change. If the change occurs under these conditions it is a gift, never an act of calculation; it is a small sign of love, no more or less—and that's a lot! After the answers to the check-in question, it is time to end the session and let the couple leave together, making a new appointment within a few weeks.

The counselor may say: "I congratulate you because you have discovered meaningful goals for both of you to develop further, and I wish you success in your endeavor. And don't forget: There won't be immediate positive results. First there is a tunnel you have to go through, and later, when you have succeeded in passing through this tunnel of bad habits, and old wounds are still bleeding, then perhaps the sun will shine again in your family, and the wounds will close forever."

OBSERVATIONS FROM EXPERIENCE

My experiences with this questioning scheme have been encouraging. These observations are worth noting:

- Most partners know exactly what it is that upsets the other, or what changes would make the other happy. They seldom make a wrong guess. The problem of marriage conflicts is mostly not lack of information, but lack of goodwill.

- Meaning-centered family therapy strengthens the ability to self-transcend in each partner. The family member is not asked what hurts him or her but what hurts the other. The partner is directed to see the wounds of the other, and at that moment pity and compassion naturally arise. This supports the renewal of goodwill (the "will to meaning") and the readiness to take action. If, instead, the family member is asked what hurts him or her, the attention is directed to his or her own wounds. This blocks the renewal of goodwill and the readiness to do something for the other.

- Often the partner's offer of goodwill is regarded as too small and more is demanded. The counselor should not give in at this point. At the center of meaning-oriented family therapy are not the demands on the other but the vision of improved behavior demanded from oneself—demands for no other purpose than to save the partnership, which is a high value.

- Even if only one partner changes behavior in a meaningful way, the hope for the whole family increases. I have had cases when one partner was not ready to change for the sake of the other, but the other was ready to do so. When both came to the next therapy session, however, both had changed. The goodwill of one awakened the conscience of the other who, in the end, didn't remain as unmoved as originally stated. We must keep in mind that all work done on oneself to make living together a bit easier for the other is an expression of still-existing love. The moment you receive an expression of love, it touches the heart—and who of us is unreceptive to love?

As mentioned before, logotherapists promote the overcoming of inner obstacles by helping individuals to discover meaningful goals and tasks waiting beyond the obstacles. They confront clients with the "I should" and the "I could" to evoke their feeling of responsibility. Guided by the questioning scheme described here, people discover what their "I should" is within the present family situation, and they are motivated to say "yes" to the "I could" and to jump over the inner obstacle.

As symbolized by the metaphor of the diving board, the first jump is hard. Expressing goodwill is one thing, but acting upon it without expecting immediate feedback is another. After each jump, a long fall occurs. Patients must be prepared for this. But without jumping into self-responsibility and without some period of uncertainty and loneliness, no new beginning in a partnership is attainable.

It may happen that one partner jumps, and the other doesn't. It is possible that the partnership cannot be maintained because one partner refuses to contribute at this final stage. It can happen that, in spite of therapeutic assistance, separation and divorce are unavoidable. But even then, the one who jumped to rescue the partnership is the one who will emotionally better survive its breakdown. Because once one has jumped (which means, developed further), one will be able to do so again, to overcome new obstacles and, if need be, to master life alone.

Goethe wrote: "Also from stones thrown onto your path something magnificent can be built." Obstacles inside and outside of us are also material to build a monument of dignity.

QUESTIONING SCHEME FOR COUNSELING COUPLES

Step I

The couple describes a conflict situation which they have gone through without solution.

Counselor: "What do you think was the actual element that upset your partner?"

Each answers.

Counselor: "Is it correct what your partner presupposed?"

If one or both fail to agree, they can correct the presumption.

Step II

Counselor: "If a similar situation occurs again, do you see any possibility to prevent your partner from getting so upset?"

Each answers.

Counselor: "Would this change of behavior your partner mentioned really help you in similar critical situations?"

If one or both fail to agree, they can describe what instead would help them, but they are not allowed to make greater demands.

Step III

Counselor: "Are you ready to realize the possibility you mentioned and to change your behavior—regardless of what your partner does?"

Each answers "yes" or "no."

If only one says "yes," this may be enough to increase hope for the family.

Counselor: "Are you happy about the readiness of your partner to change him or herself a little bit? Can you accept it as genuine?"

No more discussion; end of session.

It is not necessary
to say everything
we feel and think–
harm easily may result.

When someone says:
"I hate you!"
only so he will not repress
his hatred,

and the other replies:
"You dirty dog!"
only to prove
that he expresses his thoughts,

then there exist
two offending words
which will still hurt
when they are no longer there....

Elisabeth Lukas

CHAPTER 9

Logotherapeutic Crisis Intervention:
A Case History

The following case history was told to me by Dr. Robert Barnes, head of the Department of Counseling and Human Development at Hardin-Simmons University, Abilene, Texas, one of the most knowledgeable logotherapists in the United States.

Two families, both with young girls living next to each other, were close friends. One morning one of the mothers, on her way to the supermarket, stopped at her friend's house and jumped out of the car. Leaving the car door open and without turning off the engine, she asked her friend, as she often did, if she could do any shopping for her. The other mother was pleased because she was preparing her four-year-old daughter's birthday party and needed some party snacks and decorations. The two women quickly made a shopping list.

Meanwhile, the little girl saw the neighbor's car in front of her house. Mary often had been taken along in this car, and she climbed through the left-open door. What happened next can only be presumed. The child probably released the parking brake and jumped out when the car moved. The car rolled over the girl and crushed her.

The mother came out of the house at that moment. Terrified, she rushed to the child and scooped her up in her arms. Mary, who was still conscious, looked directly into her mother's eyes while blood flowed from her nose, mouth, and ears. Then she died.

Time, in this case, was not a healer. The severe shock of the trauma was ever present. Night after night, the mother awakened, tortured by dream images in which she saw the girl's blood-drenched face, her breaking eyes focused on her mother. A therapist brought no comfort. On the contrary, searching questions into her past (for example: "Had Mary been wanted?") upset the mother to such a degree that she became hysterical in the doctor's office. The therapist quickly guided her out the back door, not wanting other patients in the waiting room to see the "scene." Meaning well, but with little tact, the therapist gave the woman the address of a suicide-prevention clinic, then returned to the office.

After this disappointing attempt at finding help, many wretched weeks passed. During the day, the woman remained passive, paralyzed by fear of the nightmares that tortured her body and soul. Then her sister, on a visit, suggested she see Dr. Barnes. "He is a counselor, working with a different method. Maybe he can help."

Reconstructing the case as closely as possible in Dr. Barnes' words:

The patient seemed numb, suffering from an inner conflict. What was it that stood between her and her ability to master her fate? One sentence, which she repeated over and over again, gave me a clue. "Why did I have to watch my girl's dying? Why did I have to witness this horrible moment that I can never forget?"

Here was the core of the tragedy, the opening through which logotherapy could enter. "My dear Ms. X," I told her. "You have suffered unspeakable pain. But I am so glad that you took your daughter into your arms. That you didn't stop, halfway to your child, frozen with terror, covering your eyes at this unbearable sight. By hugging your little one you truly enabled her to say good-bye to you. Otherwise, the last thing she saw would have been the dirty tire that rolled over her. Your action allowed her to face the eyes of her mother and read in them the love that had surrounded her all her short life."

"We can be sure that the child didn't feel pain at that moment because such severe injury deadens all sensation of the nervous system. She felt safe and secure. There is no greater security on earth, especially for a child, than in a mother's arms. Your action enabled your daughter, surrounded by motherly love, to slip from the safest shelter life has to offer to still another shelter—what a beautiful good-bye!"

"But you do have a price to pay for the gift you gave her—the price of your memory of that terrible moment of parting."

While I spoke, the woman listened attentively and seemed to find an inner peace. "You mean it was good what I did, good for Mary?" she asked, and I saw the dawn of a meaning behind the darkness of her pain. "It was the best you could do in your situation." I assured her.

"No pain, and secure in my arms," she murmured; then she straightened up. "If this is so, then I can live with the memory of little Mary's blood-covered face."

"When you see her in your dreams again, take her in your arms and cradle her once more," I told her when she left my office. My hopes were fulfilled when I learned in a subsequent follow-up session that she was able to sleep undisturbed by nightmares.

DISCUSSION

We hardly can know for certain what factors make therapy effective. Because the above case presents a relatively simple brief therapy, we can try to trace the factors that may have been effective.

Diagnosis

The first step in any therapy is the diagnosis—and the danger of a misdiagnosis. Misdiagnoses can happen when the patient's situation is under- or overvalued, which falsifies the true overall picture.

In this case, there was little danger of overvaluing the traumatic event itself, because a child's death is pretty much the worst event that a mother can experience. But Mary's death, in itself, had not caused the pathogenic disturbance in the mother, as became evident during the session. On the other hand, the woman's first therapist undoubtedly undervalued the trauma itself and searched her past for pathological elements. The therapist failed to see the real burden under which the mother broke.

Dr. Barnes avoided both mistakes. By asking the question, "What stands between the woman and the overcoming of her suffering?" he correctly assessed the situation. Her suffering (the death of her child) was surmountable, although it still was part of the pathogenesis because it had not been overcome.

The correct evaluation of the situation enabled Dr. Barnes to hear the woman's crucial sentence. Therapeutic experience shows that most patients "know" the essence of their problems, not by strictly rational or emotional knowledge, but by an intuitive grasp of what is still unfinished business. Patients rarely can use this intuitive knowledge by themselves to find the solution, but therapists are trained to connect their professional knowledge with their patients' intuitions.

Dr. Barnes, by correctly evaluating the situation, tuned in on the intuitive knowledge of the patient as she presented it to him: "Why did I have to witness this horrible moment of my child's dying?" This is a pathogenic or neurotic reaction, of which Frankl has said that the neurotic existence punishes itself by a lack of self-transcendence. Here, a mother not so much grieved for her child, but a human being raged against her fate. And exactly here, at this point of fury, the wound does not heal.

Therapy

When a person bemoans a fate, the therapist can commit either of two mistakes. The first, rather common nowadays, results from the idea that it is therapeutically necessary that patients give full vent to their pain. Unfortunately, as a consequence, the patients are often gripped by harmful self-pity. The other mistake is made when patients are aware of the vicious spiral in which they are burying themselves, but see as a remedy only the stopping of their complaints, without coming to terms with their substance.

Professor Barnes was safeguarded against both these pitfalls by his logotherapeutic background. With his statement, "I am so glad that you took your child into your arms," he abruptly ended the mother's spiral of self-pity and made transparent the meaning of the events from which she suffered. "You made it possible for Mary to part from you in love." In finding a meaningful interpretation later, the hurtful event was not removed. It was allowed to remain hurtful, but it gained the positive aspect of a sacrifice. "If this is so, then I can live with it." Self-transcendence overcame self-pity; the neurotic disturbance could dissipate.

The grief was not gone, nor was it supposed to be, for grieving over a person we have loved and lost keeps that person somehow alive. But those who can grieve without rebelling are regenerated in their sleep with its fluid borders between this and another world, where the living and the dead may visit each other.

If you are in despair, O man,
ask yourself if you have
not elevated to heaven
what belongs on earrh.

He who overvalues something
and will not let it go,
plunges to the depth
when fate demands its due.

But he who has acknowledged that loans
must be repaid,
can rejoice sincerely
even over happiness in the past.

Elisabeth Lukas

CHAPTER 10

Self-Help and Crisis Intervention

Self-help for psychological problems is desirable for several reasons. Treatment by professionals has become increasingly expensive. Self-help also makes people realize that they are not bundles of misery needing help from the outside; this attitude cripples self-initiative and leads to unhealthy self-pity. Equally harmful is the attitude, "others have made me sick, so others should make me well." One example is a person who suffers from weak muscles. A sedentary job is blamed ("others have made me sick") and, to strengthen muscles goes to a masseur ("others should make me well"). That individual doesn't consider strengthening the body by exercising every day; this solution could only be considered by those who feel responsible for their own health.

Self-help is also beneficial because it makes us think about our situation instead of being enmeshed in it; it enables us to distance ourselves from our distress. Self-distancing is an important concept in logotherapy. It shows us that we are not identical with our sickness—that we are *more* than our sickness.

For example, when individuals want to reduce their tendency to temper flareups, they have already grown a little beyond being angry people. They are no longer blindly driven by their impulses as by a current, but more able to sit ashore and watch the current, deciding they don't like it. And that's the first step: swimming against the current.

Who sits ashore and who helps whom in self-help? Logotherapists see it this way: In our noëtic dimension, which is what we *are* (our essence), we observe our psychophysical condition, which is what we *have*, and form an attitude toward it. Only in our spiritual dimension are we able to rise above the current of drives and, seeing ourselves at a distance, to take action. When we help ourselves, we face unwanted impulses and weaknesses in ourselves, which we do not have to accept, at least not without an attempt to change and overcome them.

Example: An individual who always overeats when angry. How can this unwanted behavior pattern be overcome?

1. View the impulse "anger-overeating" from the distance of the noëtic dimension;
2. See this impulse as lacking meaning;
3. Decide to take action against it;
4. Practice more meaningful reactions to frustrations.

Without the human capacity of self-distancing,[1] this would not be possible. No animal can observe itself, evaluate its behavior, and decide to act differently. The change would also be impossible for the individual if, after step 2, he or she would blame someone else for causing the anger and thus the overeating. This response would only precipitate more anger and more eating. Nor would change be possible if, after step 3, the individual ran to someone to stop the senseless overeating. Then reliance would be on the "someone" and step 4 would not be attempted.

Self-help means to work on ourselves. Yet to only concern ourselves with the self would not be fulfilling. It is part of human nature, especially our noëtic dimension, to reach beyond ourselves, to make use of our capacity for self-transcendence (Frankl, 1988, p. 31) to forget ourselves, and to help others. This makes possible, in addition to self-help, lay help: the mutual help of lay people. The potential of lay help has been explored in self-help groups. Helping others means also to help ourselves; we are no longer trapped in our own concerns. While self-help means to work on ourselves,

---

1   All references in this chapter are from Frankl, V. E. (1988/1969). *The will to meaning*. New York: Meridian. [This idea is found beginning on p. 17 in *WTM*. –Ed.]

lay help means to crawl from our snail shell and cross other thresholds; by helping others share their burdens, we lessen our own.

Of course, self-help and lay help have their limits. There are three areas of crisis intervention in which self-help approaches can be useful, at least as "first aid," although a complete cure may take longer or not be possible.

IRRATIONAL FEELINGS

Irrational feelings are exaggerated emotions, especially fear or guilt. They clearly differ from *realistic feelings*. For example, the fear of falling off a normal, well-built bridge is irrational, but the fear of an inexperienced mountain climber when attempting a difficult approach is based on reality. The thought that a colleague could become sick because we have been unfriendly is an example of irrational guilt feeling, but awareness of having hurt a colleague by an unfriendly word is an example of guilt based on reality.

Irrational feelings go beyond the event that triggered them. Irrational fears of stepping on a bridge, or guilt at the thought of having caused sickness through an unfriendly look, causes trouble without an outside reason. These fears take on a life of their own and occupy the mind of the individual with such phobic symptoms that it is impossible to think of anything else.

For such cases, paradoxical intention is indicated. Persons afraid of bridges should tell themselves how wonderful it would be to take a cool bath in the river below. "Fear of falling in?" they are instructed to say, "That's exactly what I want! I hope I'll slip and fall in; it would be a great chance to refresh myself."

Paradoxical intention is also applicable in cases of irrational guilt feelings, even if the paradoxical attitude seems a little "immoral." But one must keep in mind that we ridicule something because it must not be taken seriously or because it will undermine our health. So it is permissible for the person with irrational guilt feelings to intend to look as unfriendly as possible at all colleagues, so they will become sick and take sick leave.

The human capacity for self-distancing plays a part here. We distance ourselves from fear, which acts like a blackmailer. The more we give in, the more is demanded. We fear that we will fall into the water, and therefore avoid all bridges. The "blackmailer" threatens to send some compromising photos to a newspaper and the victim pays. The person affected by phobias keeps paying tribute to the irrational fear. There is only one way out: To laugh in the face of blackmail and ask the blackmailer to send the pictures to many papers, even to give out names and addresses: "I have always wanted to see my photo in the papers!" A victim who speaks that way to the blackmailer drives off the tormentor; there is nothing to gain from this victim, who is now safe from attack.

Example of how self-help and crisis intervention may be initiated by a single letter:

> Dear Dr. Lukas, here is my problem: My father, who was a choir director, had a long-standing affair with a singer. Our family, especially my mother, suffered greatly. My husband and I also sang in that choir, so when we moved to another town it was a welcome reason to quit.

> My husband joined the choir of our present town and asked me to join, too. I have an unexplainable fear of doing this. My husband laughs it off as "menopause trouble" (I am 54). Recently the fear has grown so bad that I have asthma every time my husband goes to rehearsal, even though I have no reason to suspect that he goes because of another singer. I have the feeling that sooner or later it will happen. I get so angry that I fear our marriage will suffer. I have read your books but haven't found the magic word. I guess right now I don't have the necessary sense of humor for paradoxical intention. Please help.

The logotherapeutic response:

> Dear Mrs. X, you realize quite correctly that paradoxical intention could free you from your excessive attention to a situation in which you feel trapped. This insight is valuable because it shows you are aware there is no real threat.

> Before using paradoxical intention, I would recommend two corrections in your attitude. First, that you simply forgive

your father for what he did wrong in his life. This is a matter between him and his conscience. Forgive him and close this chapter of your "childhood." Second, do not link your father's behavior with that of your husband. Your husband is a person in his own right with unique strengths and weaknesses. You do him an injustice when you see your father in him.

After you have accomplished these two inner corrections, you can fight your jealousy and fear with some paradoxical formulations by wishing him many young attractive singers who will hang onto his neck and gobble him up. You will see he will always come home in one piece. You will also see that genuine love dissolves fear, sadness, and anger. Love is not concerned with the self but with the partner.

Reaction of patient:

Dear Dr. Lukas, thanks for rescuing me with your quick answer. It is so simple that I am surprised I didn't think of it myself. I feel better already and will continue thinking in that direction.

ESCAPE FROM DEPENDENCY

The above case also illustrates a second area where self-help is applicable. It illustrates the strange idea of a fateful dependency: "This is what happened to mother, so it will happen to me, too."

The cause-and-effect result that exists in the physical and psychological area is an illusion in human relationships. If I cut my finger, it will bleed. If I am humiliated, I'll be sad. These are cause-and-effect situations. But "because my father cheated, I mistrust my husband," or "because my wife left me, I drink," are excuses for freely made decisions which could just as well have been made differently.

In the noëtic dimension we are never completely dependent on physical, psychological, or social events. We are free to decide what to do with our bleeding finger, how to deal with sadness caused by humiliation, and how to live with a miserable childhood or the loss of a partner. To ask about the causes of psychological upsets and wrong behavior are wrong questions because our decisions about how we live are not determined by causes but by ourselves—in the face of the causes.

No cause forces us to drink, smoke, look at TV, or cling to others, even if our horoscope says so, our childhood was without love, or our biorhythm shows a low. The only thing that forces our decision is our belief in dependency.

Belief can move mountains, and the belief in dependency moves them right in front of our door, which can no longer be opened and traps us within the four walls of our dependency. The countermeasure is to gather the healthy resources of the human spirit and to recapture our freedom of choice. Just as humor drives away irrational fears, so defiance frees us from the chains of self-made dependencies.

Regaining freedom of decision has its price, in that we must give up something: the security of old thought patterns and habits, some short-term benefits in favor of long-term goals, or the comfort of the status quo in order to take risks.

An example follows of how self-help can be initiated in situations of such presumed dependency, illustrated through an exchange of letters:

Letter from Norbert to his parents:

Hello Mom, hello Pop, the attorney probably called you and told you where I am. In the clink again. Probation was called off because I quit therapy. So I failed again. And it looked good for a while, the job training and so on. And now?

I don't want to write about that. I'm so stupid. The city ruined me. Jobs here and there, but the money was soon gone. I wanted to be strong, free, a Rambo. I failed in everything but I wouldn't admit it. Kept pretending, made big plans. I couldn't come home, not even phone. Why now? The mask is off. I'm a pile of shit.

I know, Mom, you go to the mailbox looking for a letter. You expect an explanation. I know you don't understand me—but what can I explain if I don't understand myself?

Am I really so helpless that someone always has to tell me what to do? And then I resist it. You know that. Oh, shit! Here I am crying. I'm afraid. But what good does it do now? I must see what I can make of myself. At last I must succeed. Or?

Please no sermons, don't condemn me, and most of all, don't blame yourselves. You have done everything for me, really. It's damn hard to write this letter. I don't know what you think of me now. Also I need a few things from home. I'm looking forward to your reaction.

My letter to Norbert:

Dear Norbert, you will be surprised to get a letter from an unknown person. Your mother is a client of mine and showed me your letter. She asked for help. I would like to try because your letter shows so many positive and hopeful signs.

First, I want you to see that your description of your situation has two levels. First, there is Norbert, the failure. He quit therapy, has not written home, has worn a mask and lived by illusions and pretensions. He is difficult to understand, is dependent and immature. One must be afraid of him and for him. All this is in your letter.

But there is another level, the "real" Norbert. The essence of Norbert. What do we know about him? He is angry at the other Norbert and tears off his mask. He has courage, admits mistakes. He thinks of his parents who check the mailbox every day, and he contacts them. He wants to be independent and act responsibly, he wants to make something of himself. And he is able to do it, because he can manage difficult things, such as writing a letter, that is "damn hard" to do.

So there are these two Norberts in one person, and they fight with each other. Who will win? Will the "real" Norbert surrender to "Norbert, the failure"? Or will he grow beyond the weak Norbert and become the person he was meant to be when he was born? Perhaps make the world a little better place?

Everything is still possible, nothing has been decided. And no one will decide *for* you. Only you can decide which Norbert will win. But please know that I keep my fingers crossed for the "real" Norbert and wish you all the strength.

Response from Norbert two months later:

Your letter really surprised me and made me think because you have hit the nail on the head. I first resented that Mom showed you my letter, but now I see it was good she did.

I want to thank you for your concern and tell you that your letter helped me several times when I was ready to give in. I'm amazed that you care. That honors and strengthens me, the "real" Norbert. I'm glad to tell you that I have decided to go back to therapy in a drug counseling center. I've made up my mind to win the fight against myself. I know there are difficulties ahead, so please keep your fingers crossed....

REGAINING WELL-BEING

In my letter, besides my challenge to a healthy defiance, I hinted at meaningful tasks waiting for him in the world. My intention was to tap the human capacity for self-transcendence. To the extent that we forget ourselves and become involved in a task, we feel well, just as a child, submerged in play, is happy. In contrast, our well-being suffers when we feel superfluous, with no tasks. Then people may become sick, even suicidal.

In affluent societies, our continuous demands for more and more leads to constant frustration. It begins in school, when children expect good grades without any effort on their part. It continues with adolescents who don't appreciate what is being offered to them in sports, hobbies, and entertainment and become bored consumers of "fun," not knowing what to do with their leisure time. As adults, they are not satisfied with their economic and social progress but wish to "self-actualize" themselves. And older adults, not grateful about their extended life span, grumble about a world they no longer understand. Of course, these are generalities, but they show a trend that breeds crises, causes dissatisfactions, and reduces the feeling of well-being.

I am not saying there are no grievances to be expressed. But protest needs to be balanced by gratitude for what is good in this world. We have no constitutional right to lead a long, happy, healthy life. That is a gift. We can choose our actions and attitude, but much of what we face is fate—a friendly fate for which we can be grateful, or an unfriendly one which, if unavoidable, we have to accept and, by thinking of still worse alternatives, find a new attitude.

A Jewish joke often told by Frankl makes that point. A man goes to a rabbi to complain about his impossible situation: with a wife and four children, he lives in one small room. The rabbi advises him to take in a goat and come back in a week. The man returns in desperation: "We cannot stand it; the goat stinks." The rabbi advises him to take the goat back to the stable and come back in a week." The next week the man beams. "Life is wonderful! No goat—only we six!"

A case history shows that gratitude can be kindled even in tragic circumstances: An elderly patient came to me with psychosomatic complaints. Any change of weather caused unbearable pain that even strong medication could not relieve. His past had been traumatic. During the last months of the War, when he was 13, his mother was killed. His father had died at the war front. The boy was beaten and both legs broken. They healed but not in the anatomically correct position. After the war he learned a simple profession, married, and had two sons. His pains began when his sons became independent and his wife left him.

While he told his story he wept. He felt betrayed by fate. "I haven't prayed for 30 years," he confided, "but now I wonder if I should ask God at least to give me a pain-free old age."

This was my cue. "You know what," I suggested. "Before you ask for something, start with thanks." The patient stared at me in disbelief. "Yes," I told him, "in the evening, when you lie in bed and look back on your life, tell God, or yourself: 'In 1945, during the last months of the war, I could have died by a thousand coincidences. I lived. For that I am grateful.' Then, close your eyes and surrender yourself to sleep. The next evening, in bed, tell yourself: 'For 13 years I had a mother, a good mother. For this I am grateful.' And again close your eyes and go to sleep. The following evening tell yourself: 'In my childhood I went through a cruel time. They broke my legs but they didn't break me. I could work and support my family. For this I am grateful.' And continue in that vein on other evenings."

A few weeks later, I met the patient again. He looked well. "Isn't it strange," he said. "My pain is gone or at least is bearable although I haven't even started with my prayers."

Well-being has less to do with outer circumstances than we might expect. It has much to do with gratitude for that great gift, "life," and for the meaning life offers to each one of us. It is good to remember that life doesn't lose its meaning under any circumstances, not even the most difficult and painful ones. In every situation, it is possible to discover its inherent meaning potential. The way out of an emotional low leads up the rungs of a ladder resting on the ground of fundamental gratitude and reaching into the high level of life tasks waiting to be fulfilled.

THE PLACE OF SELF-HELP

Professionals have their place in crisis intervention. But so do self-help and lay help. The pastor is not the only good Christian, and the trained counselor is not the only good "helper." On the contrary, both may fail in day-to-day life while the lay person, using common sense, may succeed. Here are a few basic rules for success:

- Don't take irrational feelings and fears seriously; defuse them with humor and paradox.

- Don't give in to presumed dependencies; defy them with a deep conviction that humans in essence are free.

- Be thankful for the gifts of life because nothing can be taken for granted; much of our good fortune we notice only when it is lost.

Humor, healthy defiance, and thankfulness are great life supports, and help us out of crises and sickness—and this comes entirely from our own strength! True helping professionals will not hesitate to pass on this bit of wisdom so that individuals may be more in touch with their own resources.

An obstacle on the path,
it towers to the sky...
A wanderer stands before it,
and while he looks at it,
anxious, hesitant, terrified,
he lifts his eyes up to the sky.

He has traveled from afar,
dust is on his shoes...
He has passed places, people,
forests, meadows,
bent over his staff—
much he has seen,
but never the sky.

Now he stands still, depressed,
perplexed, helpless, lonely...
But suddenly he smiles,
deeply touched by an insight.
Had there been no obstacle here,
he realizes, I'd have never
seen the sky.

Elisabeth Lukas

CHAPTER 11

Personal Attitudes and the Preservation of Life

Viktor Frankl was a witness to a century that is arguably among the darkest in human history. But his "yes to life," in spite of all that he experienced, is one of the tiny rays of light that penetrated the 20th century. It is on this ray of light I want to focus so it may warm our hearts and unconditionally confirm life, and thus preserve it.

This is important because the preservation of life, especially human life, has become threatened. Such preservation depends on many factors, one of which is perhaps most significant. It reminds me of a sentence by Leo Tolstoy: "What you think of today, you will do tomorrow." Expressed in more general terms: The attitude we take towards life today leads to our actions of tomorrow. Our attitude to life will determine, in the last analysis, our preservation of life.

That's why it is worth thinking a bit about the special phenomenon of our *inner attitude*. Our basic frame of mind, our fundamental disposition, our viewpoint is the basis of our world view, the perspective from which we fit ourselves into our world. The phenomenon is special because it is specifically human. I know of no other living creature that is able to separate itself from the web of circumstances and to assume a personal attitude toward them. The palm tree does not assume an attitude toward its palmness, nor a shepherd dog toward its shepherd dogness. But the personality of each individual is the result of that person's inner attitude, which he or she has developed and which helps with reflection and evaluation of life experience and existence.

Research in behavior therapy has confirmed these logotherapeutic insights. One example is found in the work of Martin E. P. Seligman, who 50 years ago coined the concept of *learned helplessness*. Since then, Seligman has modified his theory in the sense that he considers the learning factor less important than he originally had thought. "More important than what happens to us," he writes, "is the manner in which we see the situation. Our attitude is significantly influenced by how we explain an event."[1] But how do people explain an event of which they become aware? They do it from the spiritual support—or lack thereof—they have in their minds.

The question of spiritual support concerns many people today. Much of today's observable wavering between a resigned mood of world cataclysm and a visionary mood of a new age is an expression of this concern. The wave of the feeling of meaninglessness, which we all have experienced at one time or another, consists of single droplets that say: "All is in vain, nothing helps, we are powerless, victims of our society and our inner drives; it does not matter what we feel and think." Stated in one sentence, the idea is: *Everything is meaningless, because nothing supports us.*

How can we find the way to a "yes to life" from such an attitude? If nothing supports us, we live unsupported; if life is seen as meaningless, it is not worth living. To be in a spiritual sense supported or not supported becomes indeed a question of "to be or not to be."

We have linked the chances of life preservation with the quality of our inner attitudes, and these, in turn, with our spiritual support. This link is new in human evolution. Life developed for millions of years without creatures being asked whether or not they wanted to live. They lived as a matter of course, just as they accepted as a matter of course that they could not decide about their living or not living. For these creatures, who

---

1   Trotter, R. J. (April, 1987). "Hilflosigkeit kann man verlernen." *Psychologie heute.*

were not capable of making decisions, the decisions were made elsewhere; nature, so to speak, advanced them a credit of a "yes to life."

Gradually, these creatures of life evolved into creatures of spirit: human beings, capable of choice. Now, the advance that nature has given us seems to have been used up; perhaps it is a characteristic of the human spirit that it doesn't need such credits. Regardless, the "yes to life" must now be expressed willingly, personally, intentionally... not only on a global plane but by each person, every day anew. Human beings not only *must* express this "yes," *they are able to do it*—for the first time in evolution, a creature is capable of saying "yes to life." And nothing can smooth the tremendous wave of meaninglessness but the capacity to say "yes" to values that are worth confirming, and to make use of this capacity.

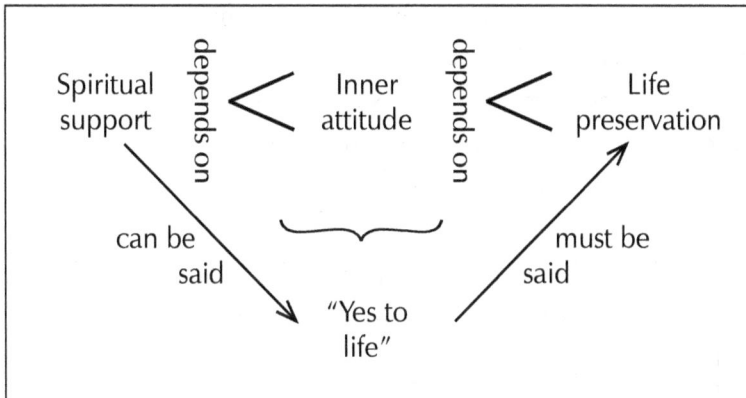

This capacity to say "yes" is not merely the reverse of the capacity to say "no." It is in some way its precondition. Just as a shadow cannot exist by itself but only in combination with the sun, namely as its nonsunny variant, and just as nonsense cannot exist by itself but only in combination with sense as its contrasting variant, so the "no" does not exist by itself but only as a "no" to something that a "yes" has made impossible. "No" means exclusion.

When I said "yes" to writing down this article, I also said "no" to everything else I could have done during the same time. When I said "yes" to my profession, I also said "no" to all other professions I could have trained for. The "no" deals with the rest of the possibilities, after we have said "yes" to one possibility. Therefore the "yes" precedes the "no," as the sun precedes the shadow, and sense precedes nonsense. And the capacity to say "yes" precedes the capacity to say "no."

We can observe this with psychologically ill and unstable people in two ways. First, those who cannot say "no" are also those who cannot say a credible "yes"; they accept every offer and grant every request because they dare not refuse, but have no inner commitment to the accepted offer and to the granted request. As a consequence, they break down sooner or later under the burden of this contradiction.

On the other hand, those who can only say "no" are in truth those who are caught in a condition in which they cannot say either "yes" or "no," and therefore cannot even manage a credible "no." These are, for instance, people who want to study but only know what fields of study are out of the question. Such people lack for successful studies a genuine "yes" for a certain subject, and lack for a successful start in a trade a genuine "no" to their studies. They sit between two chairs, as the saying goes.

Individuals who:		In truth:
Cannot say "NO"	⟶	Cannot say "YES"
Can only say "NO"	⟶	Can say neither "YES" or "NO"

It is therefore the task of logotherapy to strengthen our ability to say "yes," which after eons of evolution has suddenly been given to us. This is the basis for a "yes to life" and, if need be, a "yes to life in spite of everything." Because it relates to our capacity for making decisions and directs our lives, individually and collectively, I will now summarize the pertinent insights in logotherapy on this subject.

The most significant insight is this: *Human decisions are free acts of will that cannot be fully explained.* That means that a "yes" which could not also be a "no," is not a genuine "yes." A man who collapses because of his weak metabolism, did not say "yes" to his collapse because he had no chance to say "no" to it. A decision that can be explained by a necessity, is not a free decision.

When the Swiss psychologist Alice Miller stated that mistreated children can only become mistreating adults, she explained the mistreatments by adults through their childhood experiences, just as the collapse is explained by the weak metabolism. But as soon as the mistreatments are explainable, they are no longer based on decisions. A person, who *must* mistreat because of drives or psychological impulses does not decide for or against a specific mistreatment. Every explanation wipes out any decision-making and every decision therefore presupposes a certain amount of inexplicability. (Here theologians speak of the "mysterium iniquitatis.")

Logotherapists cannot agree completely with Alice Miller. Karl Jaspers already defined human existence as a "deciding existence" in contrast to the "driven existence" of animals.

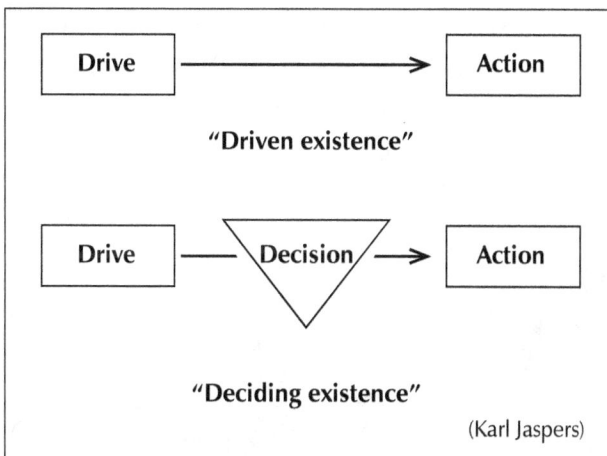

The same difference also characterizes the difference between the concepts of Viktor Frankl and Alice Miller. According to logotherapy, human beings possess a "switch" located between their drives and their actions, and this switch interrupts the automatic circuit between psychological impulses and actions. This switch presents the human decision for or against the transforming of a psychological impulse into a human being.

This is not to deny the power of drives and the force of the unconscious. Logotherapists, however, focus attention on the place where this power and this force meet with our specifically human phenomenon, our free will. We know that, among persons who mistreat others, are some who have not themselves been mistreated as children. Because they do not fit Miller's explanation, it is presumed that these individuals refuse to admit their childhood traumas and have repressed them. Logotherapists don't believe this. Rather, we believe that a human being can decide to mistreat even without a corresponding childhood experience. We also know of persons who were abused as children, even severely, but who do not harm anyone. They may be labelled inhibited in their aggression, but we also have our doubts regarding this conclusion. A person can decide not to abuse others in spite of strong psychological impulses and drives (not only because of an inhibition or block, which again would be an explainable force), because of an unexplainable act of free will.

Surprisingly, there hardly exists today one "psychology of the will," although there are quite a few "psychologies of the drives." This is so, although the will is the specifically human phenomenon, especially *the will to meaning*, as Frankl emphasized. Even human religiosity, which may be termed the "will to ultimate meaning," has been explained through the

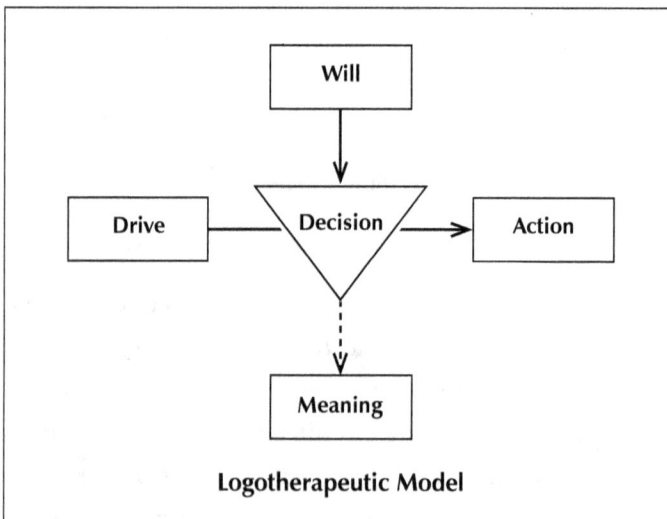

Logotherapeutic Model

dynamics of drives; for example, Carl Jung understood the human being as pushed and forced to a belief in the divine by mythical primordial impulses, the archetypes. Genuine religiosity however, is one we have chosen, not one to which we are driven, as Frankl maintained.[1] True faith is always the result of decision, never forced *upon*—nor even forced *by*—a collective unconscious heritage.

I would like to illustrate the dangers with one of the many psychological theories that exclude the human capacity to make decisions. A participant of one of my seminars reported that he had read in a professional book (that was also the basis of a television series) that the percentage of children who die as the children of widows, is a fraction higher than that of children with two living parents. The book explained this by arguing that widows are hit so severely by the loss of their partner that they unconsciously wish the death of their children, who often make the mother's relationship with a new partner more difficult. The children feel the mother's rejection and, again unconsciously, grieve to an extent that their immunity is lowered. The participant added that he had lost faith in humankind as a result of reading the report.

I suggested to him to lose faith, instead, in the absolute validity of statistical interpretations. Rather, he should carefully examine the view of human nature behind such interpretations. It seems more likely that the small percentage of fatherless children is in greater danger because the remaining family will find it difficult to make a living. Single mothers who have to work cannot always watch over their children; thus, their children have to provide for themselves with all the risks involved in such a situation. That even a negligible portion of widows wished their children to die, consciously or unconsciously, is extremely unlikely. On the contrary, it is more likely that the love for the dead partner is transferred to the children.

Let's examine the view of human nature that lies behind the death-wish theory. We discover here the same false conclusion as in Alice Miller's

---

1   Frankl, V. E. (1979). *Der unbewußte Gott, (5th ed.)*. Munich: CKösel, p. 59. [In English, see Frankl, V. E. (2000). *Man's Search for Ultimate Meaning*. Chapter 6: "Unconscious religiousness."]

mistreatment theory. It says that evil is nothing but the *automatic reaction to previously experienced evil.* Mistreated children become mistreating adults. Mothers who lost their husbands lose emotional contact with their children. Evil is passed on: I do unto you what you did unto me, regardless of whether or not the two "yous" are the same.

If we reverse the fallacy, we get an equally doubtful testimony. If evil done is the automatic reaction to evil experienced, then the good is also nothing but the *automatic reaction to the good experienced.* In the first case, personal guilt is being theorized away; in the second, personal achievement equally becomes a victim of a theory. Lost are the tremendous potentials in human beings to react to kindness with malice, or to react to evil with kindness—not automatically and unconsciously, but as a conscious decision.

Not without reason did Frankl emphasize a therapy that replaces the unconscious protest of a neurotic patient with a conscious decision in his case histories.[1] He knew that human beings, if they have a minimum of spiritual maturity, are not blindly reactive but are acting beings whose

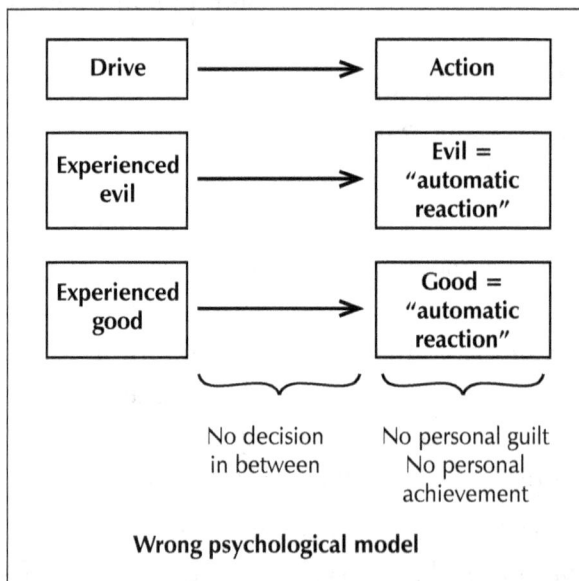

---

1   Frankl, V. E. (1983). *Theorie und Therapie der Neurosen, (5th ed.).* Munich: Reinhardt, p. 132. [In English, see Frankl, V. E. (2004).*On the theory and therapy of mental disorders.* New York: Brunner-Routledge.]

actions in the world primarily reflect inner attitudes rather than outside stimuli. In logotherapy, the old "stimulus-response" paradigm is replaced by an "attitude-action" paradigm that brings the Tolstoy sentence into sharper form: Action results from attitude. The point to remember is that we cannot choose the stimuli from outside, but we always can choose our inner attitude toward them.

The discussion of my theme first centered around two questions that in some way need to be raised with all those searching for meaning and help. The questions were:

1) Is the human being capable of making decisions?

2) Is life worth making a positive decision for it?

Let us be clear about this: Only if we can say "yes" to both these questions, a philosophically and anthropologically well-founded "yes" that cannot be doubted, only then shall we convincingly protect our lives, the lives of others, and life in general from planned or thoughtless destruction. The "yes to life" is a conviction resting on the twofold foundation of the human ability to choose and the value of life which merits our choosing it.

We have now explored the first question about our capacity to choose. The logotherapeutic answer is that human decisions have to be seen as unexplainable, free acts of will, because any explanation would negate the freedom of decision. I want to add that, for these free acts of the will, there are *no causes; rather, there are only reasons.*

Because human decisions are not explainable by causes, they are not "caused." They are guided by our will but not wantonly. Wantonness is the consequence of caprice rather than of the will. True decisions of will and faith, however, are based on reasons; that is, meanings. They represent a voluntary "yes" to someone or something, who or which is their intentional object and reason. Such reasons, in contrast to causes, explain not *what* we do but *what we do it for*—the meaning.

A simple example. A person has several kinds of fruit at home of which only a part can be eaten each day. The favorite fruit happens to be the one that keeps longest. An animal would have no choice in this situation.

It would devour the favorite fruit, regardless of whether the other kinds would be spoiled the next day. Behind the "want" of the animal stands a "must," dictated by instincts and drives. This is different for humans, as Frankl demonstrated. For humans, there stands no unconscious "must" behind the "want," but there stands a conscious "ought" *before* the "want." A human being considers what ought to be done, i.e., whether it is meaningful to let the fruit rot in a world of widespread starvation. And if there is a recognition that this ought not to be done, there is a reason for eating the favorite food last, and the easily spoiled fruit first.

Human action in such a situation cannot be explained by a "must," nor is it arbitrary, but it is directed by an "ought." The person in our example can, of course, decide against the "ought." The favorite fruit can be eaten first and the rest discarded. There exists freedom to act against meaning. But then the innate will to freedom must be repressed, even violated; he or she must say "yes" to something that deep within resists the "yes," simply because it is not worthy of the "yes." This creates the potential of conflict and a source of dis-ease, similar to those individuals who do not have the courage to say "no," instead saying "yes" to things they do not want to do.

Here is an opening for a therapeutic application much needed at the present. What is needed is a *confronting therapy*, such as logotherapy, that confronts us with a meaningful "ought," and an *evocative therapy*, such as logotherapy, that evokes the will to meaning, which often has been suppressed. Only when we no longer see ourselves and our decisions as fully explainable and caused and begin to look for reasons for our actions, for reasons to which we, from our deepest will to meaning, can say "yes," only then will we be on our way to life, to a good life.

Only when adults who were mistreated as children consider whether they *ought* to pass on their suffering to innocent people, only when widowed mothers consider whether they *ought* to deprive fatherless children of the love of their mother as well, only then will they discover genuine reasons for actions that contradict the negative psychological prognoses. Only then will they actualize values that ought to be actualized not only in spite of their own problems but even because of them.

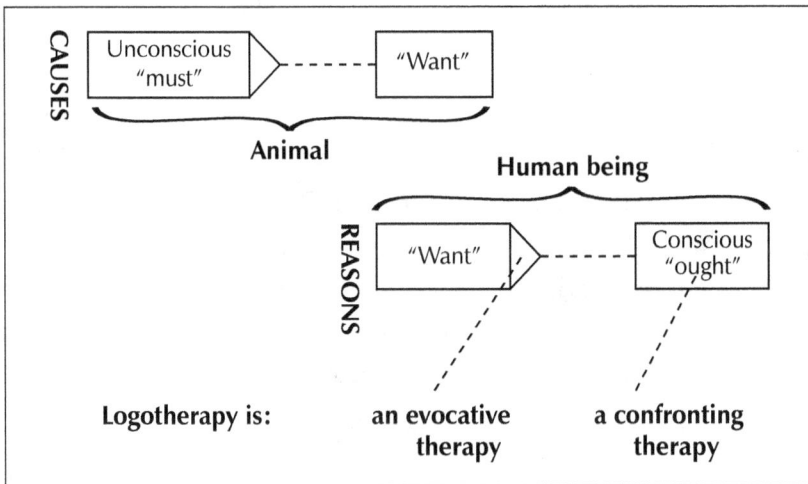

Human decisions are made for reasons, they go for the "ought" or against the "ought," for the meaningful or against the meaningful. It is not the task of the therapist to define the "ought," to prescribe the meaningful, as Frankl put it, but to develop and to strengthen the patient's capacity to say "yes," and to deal with the question of what is worth saying "yes" to.

Here we come to the second question: *Is life worthy of affirmation, and why?*

I would like to insert an episode from my own life. The year was 1976. In Germany abortion was made legal in situations of social distress, with the stipulation that pregnant women, before abortion, receive advice about possible help if they decided to have the child. I was at that time a clinical psychologist in a public counseling center, and was assigned to counsel such pregnant women.

I did not mind this field of counseling, which was meant to be pro-life, but the activity deeply depressed me. The more I talked to women who wanted an abortion, the more I realized how little the social distress factor had to do with their wish. It may be different in countries outside of Germany, but there were mortgages to pay off, the expenses of their own development and studies, the disinclination to raise an additional child, the threat to self-actualization. Probably at no time was I lied to as much as then; too many decisions against the growing life were not based on genuine social distress.

The case I want to report was an exception. Here everything was true, the situation of the young pregnant woman was really difficult, her despair understandable. She already had four children in a much-too-small apartment, her husband was unemployed, hot-tempered, addicted to alcohol, and he did not support her in any way. He had even physically abused her. I must admit that I was not certain how I would have decided in her place, so dark did the future of this family appear.

I was all the more surprised when the young woman came back the day after our counseling session. She had received the medical permission and could have gone to the hospital. But she came, she told me, because she had felt my concern and because something had happened that she wanted to discuss with me. When she had returned from our interview, her husband had told her that he had just found work, and he also firmly promised her to do something about his alcoholism.

"Do you think," she asked me, "this is a hint from above to give birth to the child?" This was one of the moments when we are asked, not as a professional but as a human being. I answered spontaneously: "If this is the way you see it, that's the way it will be." After a few minutes she made the decision to say "yes" to the budding new life.

I continued to counsel the woman for an entire year until I moved to Munich. During this year, her husband agreed to disulfiram therapy and came to family counseling, both of which were successful. He worked in the freezing department of a food factory and received gifts of food to supplement the diet of his family. The three older children were accepted in a kindergarten, relieving the mother. The new baby was a darling little boy, who was received with love and joy. At the same time, the social agency allocated a larger apartment to the family.

It was amazing for me to see how everything turned out for the better, after I had witnessed the despair of the young woman—after I had been uncertain! I am almost tempted today to ask a similar question as the young woman had asked me: "Do you think this was a hint from above, never to doubt an unborn life and its chances?"

If this is so, I experienced another "hint," although in a different direction. I became witness of a moving incident, described in one of my German books.[1] Briefly, it concerns a dying patient who had to spend her last hours motionless in her bed, and yet was able with a few whispered sentences to achieve long-lasting benefits for another person. This proves that an artificial shortening of her life, of even a few hours, would have deprived her and the other person of a positive possibility, which would have been irretrievably lost. For we can never be sure that *something may not be waiting for each person*: for the child, perhaps, an important work as an adult, or a love to give out, even though not much was received as a child; for the person who is incurably ill, a last reconciliation or a message to his or her family to make a good parting still possible, in spite of everything. This does not mean that we have no responsibility for judicious family planning for the entry into life, and for medical help to relieve pain at the end of life. It *does* mean that quantity and quality of life *expectations* can be no criteria for or against life *destruction*.

Wolfgang Zander, a professor at the University of Munich, pointed out that there is a significant difference between hope and expectation. While expectation has a demand quality, hope contains trust in positive possibilities. He maintained that, in our times, a decisive shift has taken place from an attitude of *hope* toward *expectation*. Today, people hope less and expect more than in previous times. This is even expressed in our use of language. In former times we said of a woman who was pregnant that she was "of good hope"; today, we say that she is "expecting."

Returning to an earlier thought: There is hope for every human life that it can still be filled with meaning even when the expectations for this life can be fulfilled only partly or not at all. We do not know the eventual goal of evolution, but there is hope that it follows a meaningful—though to us unclear—plan whose realization is worth saying "yes."

---

1 Lukas, E. (1986). "Sinn hat jedes Henscheflleben" in *ABC des Lebensglucks* (P. Raab, ed.). Freiburg: Herder.

Here I am, back at my original argument. After eons of unconscious life that was unable to make decisions, the bearers of life have evolved into bearers of spirit, human beings with consciousness and the capacity to choose. The question arises: Does this retrospection not justify the conjecture that all life was charged with developing a field where the spirit could find expression, and that this field may be the biophysical basis of human existence?[1] Whereby the dimensional superiority is shown in the fact that the spirit is of a different nature than its field of expression, just as the phenomenon of light is of a different nature than the generators, cables, and switches in the wall. Of course, we cannot light a room with a defective switch, but in this case the light bulb is not defective, it simply cannot be turned on by means of the switch. It cannot show its existence which, however, is there—independent of any switches.

In the same manner, logotherapy defines the noëtic dimension as something that itself cannot become ill but needs the services of a healthy organism to reveal itself. The spirit, therefore, is also seen as something that cannot die but, as far as we know, has no field to express itself except in union with the biophysical.[2] Seen in this manner, the entire human culture cannot be interpreted in merely psychoanalytical terms as the *progressive taming of the animalistic in the human being*, but also must be seen as the

---

The spiritual dimension of the human being

- cannot become ill
- cannot die
- exists beyond time and space
- seeks specific expression in space and time
- needs a field in which to express itself
- this field is the living organism

The will to meaning = the will to living

---

1   Frankl, V. E. (1984). *Der leidende Mensch, (2nd ed.).* Bern: Huber, p. 109.

2   Ibid, p. 134.

evolution of the human spirit that we know as the *traces of the spirit in space and time.*

We may assume that spirit exists nowhere within our body, that it exists beyond space and time, but has its effects and leaves its traces there, and therefore requires a close connection with the human organism. From this viewpoint, we have a further reason to keep hold of the human organism as far as possible. It "contains" a spiritual person, developed or not developed, blocked or not blocked by physical defects; the body "contains" the spirit—although not in a spatial sense—and the spirit seeks specific expression in this world. Who would dare to deprive the spirit of a unique person its opportunities for such a unique expression, perhaps its last ones?

As stated earlier, nature has advanced a credit to all living creatures to say "yes" to life in the form of the drive for self-preservation. For us as creatures endowed with the gift of spirit, this credit has lost its significance, because the spirit does not submit to psychological drives. But let us not forget that creatures so endowed also have received that ability to see a goal worthy of "yes." Not the demand of a *must*, but the awareness of an *ought*—our will to meaning.

Now all depends on the endeavor of parents to awaken this will in their children, on the ability of teachers to advance this will in their pupils and students, on the courage of therapists to include this will in the therapy of their patients… and on our readiness, every one of us, to follow this will day by day.

The will to meaning is the will to living.

I would like to see
a piece of reality
in all its dimensions.

Everything there is:
Day and Night,
Proximity and Distance,
Truth and Error,
Pain and Grace,
Joy and Sorrow—

But who will decide
what chance
will select for me?

I have seen
a piece of reality
in all its dimensions.

Everything was there:
Good and Evil,
Light and Dark,
Quiet and Restlessness,
Being and Not-being,
You and Me—

But the details
I selected
were my decision.

Elisabeth Lukas

www.ingramcontent.com/pod-product-compliance
Lightning Source LLC
Chambersburg PA
CBHW052135270326
41930CB00012B/2897